James A. Simpson is a ⌷⌷⌷⌷ ⌷⌷⌷⌷⌷⌷ ⌷⌷ ⌷w
that he had his primar⌷ ⌷⌷⌷⌷⌷⌷⌷⌷ ⌷ education. At
Glasgow University he s⌷⌷⌷⌷ ⌷⌷⌷⌷s and nuclear physics. He
later studied divinity at the same university, gaining not only
the gold medal in Old and New Testament Studies, but a
scholarship to study for a year in New York. After ministering
in Falkirk and Glasgow he moved in 1976 to Dornoch in the
North of Scotland to become minister of the town's
mediaeval cathedral. During his 21 years there he wrote
several books including *Holy Wit*, which for many weeks
topped the Scottish bestseller charts. Dr Simpson is a regular
contributor to magazines and newspapers, not only in
Scotland, but also in Ireland and the USA.

In 1992 he was appointed a chaplain to the Queen in
Scotland. Two years later he was elected to the office
of Moderator of the General Assembly of the Church of
Scotland. In 1995 he was awarded an honorary doctorate by
Aberdeen University.

Dr Simpson was born the same day and the same year as the
first man ever to travel in space. Whereas Yuri Gagarin
explored the frontiers of outer space, Dr Simpson continues
in his writings to explore the inner frontiers of life. In this
book, as in many of his previous books, he uses kindly
humour and many unforgettable stories to shed light on the
meaning of life and love.

LIFE, LOVE AND LAUGHTER

'*Life, Love and Laughter* is packed with anecdotes ... the Very
Rev Dr J.A.Simpson has found the way to lift the spirits with
real laughter.'

— Cameron Simpson, *The Herald*

BY THE SAME AUTHOR

There Is a Time to...
Marriage Questions Today
Doubts Are Not Enough
Keywords of Faith
Holy Wit
Laughter Lines
The Master Mind
More Holy Wit
All About Christmas
The Laugh Shall Be First

Life, Love & Laughter

Vintage Wit and Wisdom

James A Simpson

Steve Savage
LONDON AND EDINBURGH

Steve Savage Publishers Ltd
The Old Truman Brewery
91 Brick Lane
LONDON
E1 6QL

www.savagepublishers.com

First published in Great Britain by Steve Savage Publishers Ltd 2002
Reprinted 2002

Copyright © James A. Simpson 2002

ISBN 1-904246-04-4

British Library Cataloguing in Publication Data
A catalogue entry for this book is available from the British Library

Typeset by Steve Savage Publishers Ltd
Printed and bound by The Cromwell Press Ltd

Contents

Foreword 7

Introduction 9

Pre-Madonna 11

Rural Matters 19

Laughing Matters 24

Family Matters 35

Food for Thought 44

Fair and Stormy Weather 59

Ho-ho-holy Humour 64

Jingle Bells 77

I Was There 83

The Later Years 93

The Feather in His Cap 99

Waste of Muscle, Waste of Brain 112

Miscellaneous Stories 120

Dedicated to

Derick, Neil, Graeme and Alistair
who love life and laugh often

Foreword

The Very Rev Dr James Simpson is one of the Church of Scotland's best-loved and most admired leaders. As a parish minister and as Moderator of the General Assembly, Jim has brought to all his tasks compassion, warmth, humour and wisdom.

He is much in demand as a preacher, after-dinner speaker, and wise counsellor. Jim and his wife Helen are true representatives of the human face of the Kirk.

As a writer too, Jim has left many of us in his debt. His pastoral books have been very helpful, and personal anthologies such as *All about Christmas*, *Holy Wit*, *Laughter Lines*, and *The Laugh Shall Be First* have been repeatedly ransacked by after-dinner speakers and his fellow ministers, myself included!

Royalties from his books have gone to Cystic Fibrosis research. This is a cause dear to Jim's heart, more especially since his granddaughter Sally suffers from this difficult and often heart-rending condition. So far from book royalties and fees from after-dinner speaking, Jim has raised around £40,000 for this worthy cause.

This latest collection of anecdotes and sayings, gathered by Jim over the years, will gladden the heart as much as his previous books have done. I often found myself laughing aloud, then thinking, 'I can use that!'

Not only will this compassionate and humorous book add to the coffers of an excellent charity, it will lift the spirits of all who read it.

Ron Ferguson

Introduction

Abraham Lincoln said, 'They say I tell a great many stories. I reckon I do, but I have learned from long experience that plain people are more easily influenced through the medium of a story or a humorous illustration than in any other way.' A good story is remembered long after abstract thoughts are forgotten.

Throughout my life I have kept a notebook – a repository of well-turned phrases, snatches of illuminating dialogue from books and newspapers, fresh ways of stating old truths, of highlighting our hopes and fears, aspirations and pretensions, and our propensity at times to mess things up. In these notebooks, I have also recorded thoughts about what I have noticed and felt at various stages in my life. These insights, anecdotes and illustrations I have later used in newspaper and magazine articles, in after-dinner speeches and broadcast talks, and in sermons, for I believe it is not enough for a speaker or preacher to be right about what he declares, he must be interesting as well. Not far from where we stay in Perthshire is the parish of Dull. Though Dull is a beautiful part of Scotland, the thought of being known as the Dull minister is not one that appeals to me.

I apologise for the apparent 'egotism' of parts of the book – the use of the first person pronoun, and the numerous references to personal experiences. I could see no way of avoiding this if I was to share stories that provided me with insights into human nature, that have comforted me and made me laugh, that have caused a lump to form in my throat and a tear in my eye. The stories are about the ordinary stuff of everyday life. For the most part I have left them to do their work in the mind of the reader unhampered by further comment. I hope some of the stories will make the readers chuckle, for laughter is great therapy. I am told it exercises the heart, thorax, abdomen, diaphragm and lungs. In our troubled and often inhuman world, a sense of humour is a great gift, part of the human survival kit. It does help preserve sanity. Because not taking ourselves too seriously is closely related to taking other things very seriously, this book is a mixture of humorous stories and anecdotes that hopefully will set the mind pondering.

The royalties from this book will go to research into Cystic Fibrosis, a debilitating disease from which my oldest granddaughter and many other young people suffer. This book being essentially a collection of stories, let me begin by recounting one about a woman who had agreed to take part in a house-to-house collection. When she explained to a pensioner that she was collecting for Cystic Fibrosis, the old lady smiled and gave her a generous donation. Later that week, the collector learned that when the old lady went back into her house, her daughter, who was visiting, asked her who had been at the door. 'Oh it was a lady collecting for sixty-five roses. I wonder why they did not just go for the hundred.'

My thanks are due to Ron Ferguson, one of Scotland's most distinguished newspaper columnists, for writing the foreword. Ron was formerly minister of St Magnus Cathedral in Orkney. My thanks are also due to the Rev Robin Stewart for his careful reading of the manuscript, and to my wife Helen, my greatest encourager and critic.

James A. Simpson

Pre-Madonna

In the pre-Madonna era in Dornoch, I used to have to explain to people where we lived. But just prior to Christmas 2000 AD, Dornoch, the County Town of Sutherland, became the focus of media attention. Photographers and television crews from all corners of the world, encamped outside the town's 13th-century Cathedral where I had ministered for 21 years. The reason for this invasion by the paparazzi was that Madonna, the Queen of Pop, had chosen Skibo Castle for her wedding to the film producer Guy Ritchie, and Dornoch Cathedral for the baptism of her son Rocco. My able successor in the Cathedral, the Rev Susan Brown, officiated on both occasions.

At the time of the wedding, I was approached by a national newspaper to pen some thoughts for the newly married couple. The editor entitled the article, 'Ten steps to happiness for Madonna and Guy'.

1. I hope all your joint decisions will be as wise as that of choosing Scotland and Dornoch for your wedding!

2. Work hard at being the right partner. That is as important as finding the right partner. A female superstar of a previous generation put it well. 'It is easy to make 20 men fall in love with you in a year, but to have one love for 20 years, that is an achievement.'

3. Though romance and physical attraction are important, character is more important. What people are, ultimately matters more than what they look like.

4. Willingness to compromise reflects strength of character, not weakness. A man who learned as a child that he could get his own way if he stamped his foot hard enough, fell in love with a girl, who had been brought up to believe that all roads lead to Rome and that she was Rome. The marriage not surprisingly was a disaster.

5. At a previously highly publicised wedding – that of Prince Charles and Lady Diana – the Bible lesson was read by the Speaker of the House of Commons. Since those present had printed orders

of service, he did not announce that the reading was from Paul's first letter to the Corinthians. After the televised service he received many letters asking for a copy of the wonderful speech he had made. What Paul wrote 2,000 years ago is still relevant. 'True love is never selfish. It is patient and kind. It is not boastful or rude.' It is that kind of caring love that keeps a marriage going and growing.

6. Verbal fighting being an inevitable part of living together, it is important that you fight fairly, that you focus on the present, not the past, that you don't drag up yesterday's failures as today's ammunition, that you avoid inflammatory words such as 'always' and 'never' – 'You are always craving the limelight'; 'You are never pleasant to my mother'.

7. 'Don't let the sun go down on your anger.' Nothing destroys a relationship quite like not speaking. Though never easy, the willingness to say sorry and forgive the hasty word are essential for a happy marriage.

8. Small things can make epochs in married life. Whereas shattering experiences, like the loss of a job, or a serious illness, can sometimes draw spouses closer together, petty annoyances, can chip away at a marriage.

9. Never take each other for granted. An unexpected 'thank you' or present, a squeeze of a hand, a hug, a timely card are all marriage enriching.

10. Marriage is more manageable when both partners have a sense of humour. I think of the husband who said, 'Sometimes I submit. Sometimes I outwit.' Humour is a wonderful solvent for the grit of irritation which often gets into the cogs of married life. What infuriating creatures we can all be at times. Kindly humour can help keep differences in perspective. When a husband was reminded by his wife that he had forgotten her birthday, he replied, 'How do you expect me to remember when you never look a day older?' Where there is kindly laughter and shared jokes, the possibility of real trouble is reduced.

These pathways to happiness apply equally to any couple setting off on the wonderful adventure of marriage.

Shortly after officiating at the Madonna wedding, Susan Brown had a week's holiday with her husband in Oxford. A member of Dornoch Cathedral, who was working at that time in theatrical production in Oxford, got them tickets for the 'French and Saunders' show. She also arranged for them to meet Dawn French after the show. Before they parted, Dawn gave Susan a beautifully wrapped box. Inside was a clerical collar, on which had been written, 'To the Vicar of Dornoch from the Vicar of Dibley'.

Life is not a laughing matter, but can you imagine having to live without laughter? Abraham Lincoln was a great admirer of the writings of the American humorists Josh Billings and Artemus Ward. When someone recently sent me one of their books, entitled *Choice Bits of American Wit*, I understood why. '*There are some laughs that come out of the mouth twisted and gritty, laughs that make you feel when you hear them, as though you were being shaved by a dull razor without the benefit of soap. I don't like a giggler. That kind of laugh is like a dandelion, a feeble yeller. There is not a bit of good smell about it. Give me rather the laugh that has music in it, the laugh that looks out of a person's eyes first, then steals down into the dimple of his cheek, then waltzes a spell at the corners of the mouth, then fills the air for a moment with a shower of silvery tongued sparks, then steals back with a smile to its lair in the heart. This is the kind of laugh I love.*'

The writer Eric Linklater recalled a school report he received. It said, 'On the whole, Eric is doing fairly well, but he is handicapped by a sense of humour.' Far from being a handicap I believe a sense of humour is an enormous asset, a divine gift. The ancients used to say that time spent laughing was time spent with the gods. Kindly laughter is the cheapest anxiety reducing experience there is. It helps preserve sanity and perspective. It

13

can clear the air as nothing else can quite do. It also has no harmful side effects. When Jack Milroy, one of Scotland's finest comedians, died, a friend said, 'Jack was a walking national health service. He dispensed more good than some chemists.' Without a sense of humour we are liable to become too intense, too solemn, too pompous. It is good for solemnity's nose to be tweaked, for human pomposity to be made to look ridiculous.

When I remarked to a very devout lady that if Christianity does not make one happy, there must be something wrong either with one's interpretation of Christianity or with oneself, she haughtily replied, 'It is not the object of Christianity to make one happy, but to make one good.' Now in one sense that is true, but it also has to be said that people who are happy are usually good, for they have less inducement to be bad. So many of the problems of our day are caused by people searching for happiness in wrong ways. Boredom is the root cause of a great deal of wrongdoing. When the cowboy Roy Rogers was asked if he had ever played a bad guy in a film, he replied, 'No, because the bad guy never sings.' There is food for thought in that. Though singing and whistling are clearly not the answer to all the problems that beset us, it is difficult to think unlovely or spiteful thoughts when we are singing or whistling a happy tune.

I find it significant that the word humour and the word humility come from the same root – *humis* – meaning 'of the earth'. The Genesis story of the Tower of Babel contains wonderful touches of divine humour. Proud men have decided to build a 'tower whose top will reach the heavens'. But God has to 'come down' to see it, so minute is it from the divine perspective.

During the seventh grinding week of the peace negotiations that finally led up to the signing of the fragile Good Friday agreement in Northern Ireland, Senator George Mitchell, the American mediator, who at that time was commuting weekly between Ireland and America, one morning surprised those present by saying, 'This morning I want us to talk about things other than politics. Let us see if we can just have a good time together.' The conversation turned to fishing, family, sports and the weather. Then someone mentioned opera. At this stage Senator Mitchell interjected. 'I love listening to opera. When I return to America and put on *La Bohème*, I know Rodolfo is going to sing the same words every time. That prepares me for my return to Belfast, because the one thing I know is that I'm going to sit here and listen to you guys saying the same thing over and over again.' The representatives on both sides actually laughed. That light-hearted remark helped break the deadlock between longtime antagonists.

On hearing that a consulting firm was to provide a cost-benefit analysis of the local symphony orchestra, a humorist, concerned to highlight the absurdities of judging everything in economic terms, suggested a possible report: 'The four oboe players have nothing to do for long periods of time, so their number should be reduced. Likewise the brass and timpani section. As all the first violins play identical notes, there is obviously unnecessary duplication. An electronic amplifier could provide increased volume. Musical scores could be drastically reduced, for no useful purpose is to be served by having the horns repeat a passage already played by the strings. Eliminating redundant passages, the total concert time could be reduced considerably, with a consequent saving on lighting and heating bills. In the unlikely event of these changes resulting in some falling off in attendance, sections of the auditorium could be closed off with further savings in heating and staff.'

One-issue people live in danger of becoming obsessed. If not careful they can become like Gatsby, whose warped personality was the price of living too long with a single dream. Although not all one-issue people lack a sense of humour, they are often not in the mood to be amused!

George Burns the entertainer said, 'If I get big laughs, I am a comedian. If I get little laughs I am a humorist. If I get no laughs, I am a singer. Believe me, when I am on the stage, I have a song ready just in case!'

Early one February, a man spotted a magnificent vase in an antique shop. Because the handle had been broken off, it had been reduced from £250 to £10. The love of his life being fond of pottery, he decided to buy it for her as a St Valentine present. He hoped she would conclude that the vase had got broken in the post. In her thank-you note, she not only thanked him for the vase, but for wrapping both parts separately.

President Harry Truman's sense of humour helped foster a scepticism not only of the actual powers of the presidency, but also of the intelligence of certain high-ranking military personnel including General Eisenhower. At the beginning of 1953, when he was about to hand over the presidential seals to Eisenhower, he remarked to an aide, 'I cannot wait for that General to get here, give an order, and find that nothing happens.'

A patient who waited an hour in the doctor's surgery was finally admitted to the consulting room. Hardly had he begun to describe his symptoms than the telephone interrupted him, so that he had to start all over again. The telephone showed no mercy. He was interrupted four more times. Finally the patient reached for his hat and headed for the door. When the doctor enquired where he was going, he replied, 'To the nearest phone box.'

A rare book has been defined as a book you lend to someone and actually get returned. Book borrowers were the bane of Sir

Walter Scott's life. He once disclosed that one of the reasons he enjoyed visiting other people's libraries was to see how many books from his own library were in theirs. When Mark Twain once asked a neighbour, who was a connoisseur of old books, if he could possibly borrow one, the neighbour replied, 'You may consult it in my library, but I cannot let you take it away.' Several weeks later the book lover asked if he could borrow Mark Twain's lawn mower. 'Certainly,' said Mark Twain, 'but you must use it in my garden.'

Though there is not much humour associated with death, yet even on such occasions incongruous things are sometimes said, and happen. A few years ago a new crematorium called Parkgrove was built near the Angus village of Friockheim. At the opening ceremony, one of the speakers expressed the hope that the new crematorium would help 'breathe new life into the community'! The local undertaker Ernest Taylor tells, in his light-hearted book *The Last Man to Let You Down*, about returning one day from a funeral which had been to a cemetery 90 miles away. It was pouring with rain. By the roadside they noticed a sailor with his kitbag, thumbing a lift. Stopping the hearse, the undertaker explained that the only three seats were occupied by himself, the driver and the minister, but if he was prepared to lie in the back of the hearse, he was welcome to do so. Shortly afterwards as they drove through a small town, Ernie said he could imagine the pedestrians saying, 'Obviously a cut-price job,' there being no coffin. When they arrived at their destination, Ernie had practically to lift the young sailor out of the hearse. As he was straightening his legs, the young lad said, 'That must be the most uncomfortable journey I have ever had.' 'Look,' said Ernie, 'you are the first person ever to come out of there and complain!'

A lady from Perthshire, who was on a shopping errand to Glasgow, got totally lost in the city. At one set of traffic lights she did not know whether to turn right or left or carry straight on.

As she consulted her map, the lights changed from red, to red-orange, to green, to orange, to red, to red-orange, to green, to orange, to red. The driver of the car behind, who had been remarkably patient, instead of hooting his horn, finally came forward and said to the flustered lady driver, 'Lassie, do none of these colours appeal to you?' When she explained her predicament, he said, 'Go through the lights, then draw into the side. When I pass you, follow me and I will take you there.' Would that more drivers were as gracious and helpful.

A painter was asked by one of his customers to paint her living room the colour of a small piece of painted wood that she had given him. Having mixed the colours to what he was sure was the desired shade, he painted part of the wall. But she was not satisfied. Three times he did this, but each time she shook her head. 'It is not quite right.' At this stage she decided to call her daughter and get her advice. While she was on the phone the painter added a little more green and started painting the wall again. When she returned to the room after her lengthy phone conversation, he held her piece of wood against the wall. She liked what she saw. It was an exact match. What she did not know was that while she was on the phone, he had painted her small piece of wood with the same paint as he had put on the wall.

When a Mrs McCulloch checked in at the airport to go to Germany to visit her husband, she was asked the usual security questions, including whether anyone had given her any packages. When she explained that her mother-in-law had given her a parcel for her husband, the ticket agent looked at her very intently and asked, 'Tell me, does your mother-in-law like you?'

Rural Matters

For 25 years John owned a little Highland shop. On retiring he went south to live with his daughter. It was not until he returned a year later that he discovered just how much he was missed. The village people became a little embarrassed when they tried to explain the gap his moving had left. It was not that he had kept the community highly organised. He had never been chairman of any committee. But he knew how to listen in a way that healed the broken heart. He knew how to encourage and make incomers feel welcome. He knew the children's names before the schoolteachers knew they existed. He coaxed them out from behind their mother's skirts with a sweetie. He was a busy man, but he kept that fact well hidden. Many thought he had nothing to do but stand and listen. They came to buy a loaf of bread, but stayed to tell their story. He knew where the community was hurting. The most touching thing about it was that he was unaware he was doing anything important. He thought people came to buy groceries. Come to think of it, so did they. But while with his hands he put tins on the counter, with his tongue he was healing, cheering, comforting.

Gordon Selfridge, the multimillionaire owner of the London department store, holidayed often in West Sutherland. On one occasion he visited the local shop in Edrachillis, a shop that sold everything from wellington boots to light bulbs to groceries. He commented to the shopkeeper how well-stocked his shop was. Then, by way of making friendly conversation, he explained that he too owned a shop where he tried to sell most things. 'You may have heard of it – Selfridges of Oxford Street.' The Highland shopkeeper admitted he had heard of it, but was not overawed. 'Ah,' he said, 'but you don't have the Post Office.' Then he added, 'You should try it. It's good for profits!' Only recently did I learn that on returning to London, Selfridge opened the Post Office in his department store!

The greeting 'Come awa' ben' has its origin in the old Highland croft houses, commonly called 'buts and bens'. The 'but' was the room into which you took strangers and official guests, like the doctor, minister or insurance agent. The 'ben' was the family room into which close and trusted friends were welcomed. How often in life it is not until you lose close friends, that you begin to realise how precious they are. The loss of friendly neighbours is a fundamental loss. It is like taking the mortar out of a brick wall. Although in a new community people nod on the street, and comment on the weather, you miss those friends with whom you could let your hair down. You miss those neighbours who were genuinely interested in the details of your holiday and family escapades, who smiled warmly when they opened the door. How quickly people feel at home in a new community depends on how soon they make friends, people to whom they can turn when needing help, and not feel a bother.

In the Highlands it has long been customary when a farmer took ill and was in danger of not getting the ploughing done in time, for his neighbours to gather at his farm in the evening with their ploughs. To add a bit of fun and interest to the ploughing, the young farmers would sometimes make a competition out of it. It was from such good neighbourliness that the annual ploughing matches developed, with their many prizes – for the straightest furrow, the best kept harness, the best groomed pair of horses, for the youngest ploughman, the most recently married and sometimes the one with the largest family! In our day tractors have for the most part replaced horses, but fortunately the good neighbourliness lingers on. On moving to the Highlands I was struck by how magnificently farmers help their neighbours when the need arises, sharing combines, balers, and even farm labourers. I quickly came to realise that if there is a distinctly Highland characteristic, it is not the Sabbath, nor the heather, nor the smell of peat fires. It is a communal life in which good neighbourliness is the great law.

By way of sharp contrast, I once heard of a Londoner who was moving home. As the removal firm carried out his belongings, the man in the adjacent apartment, whom he had never met during the seven years he had lived there, rang his doorbell. 'I am going to miss you,' he said. 'You have been such a good neighbour.' His definition of a good neighbour was obviously someone who did not trouble you or make a noise. The decline of good neighbourliness may seem a fairly inconsequential social change, ranking far behind drugs, crime and racism in the league of antisocial activities, but there is no doubt that its disappearance from some communities is a major loss, for the secret of many a life has been that of finding the right friend or neighbour at the right time.

In the Highlands in the 19th century, sheepdogs often accompanied shepherds to church. At the morning services there would sometimes be as many dogs as people. They sat through the sometimes lengthy services with commendable patience – at least until the congregation stood for the benediction. Then there was much stretching and some barking as the dogs prepared to scamper out. One congregation finally decided that the service should close in a more seemly manner. Accordingly when a visiting minister was officiating, he found all the people still sitting when he was about to pronounce the benediction. When he paused, expecting them to stand, one old shepherd looked up at the pulpit and said, 'Say awa' sir. We're a' sitting to cheat the dogs.'

As a Scottish farmer was driving to market, his horse refused to cross the ford. The farmer recalled that the last time they had travelled that road, the river had been in flood. The raging waters had frightened the animal. The horse obviously had not forgotten, for though many weeks had passed and the water in the ford was now shallow, the horse refused to budge. Pushing the horse forward, he cried, 'On you go. Your memory is better than your judgment.' That is true of people I know. Bitter memories cloud their judgment.

A Scottish piper in France, though wounded three times in a charge, went on playing his bagpipes until mortally wounded. Aware that he was dying, he asked the chaplain to convey messages to his wife and family. Just before he passed away, he whispered, 'If I could only see the Scottish hills again before I die.' What nostalgia the Scottish hills still arouse – Ben Lomond,

Ben Loyal, Suilven. What inspiration artists, poets and songwriters have drawn from the Scottish mountains. Hills speak not only of vastness, but of what is constant. There is something about the hills that floods the human spirit with a deepened respect for the Creator and the gigantic forces at work in nature.

For several hours an elderly man had been enjoying fishing a peaceful stretch of river. In the soft glow of the setting sun, the landscape was transformed into a thing of real beauty. Having caught a couple of trout, he did not bother to bait his hook again. He just sat for a while drinking in the peace and beauty of the surrounding scenery. Just then a young angler came wading up the stream. As he passed he said to the old man, 'What a waste of time. Four hours and not a nibble.' 'Yes,' said the old man, 'It is a waste of time if you are fishing just for the fish. But not if you look about you. Not if you give more than a casual look to the birds and the wild flowers and the setting sun.' Pulling one of the trout out of his bag, he said to the lad, 'Here take this. It really is not what I came for.' There was a look of amazement on the boy's face. He grinned at the fish and made to leave. But as he did so, he paused for a moment to smell a wild flower.

A Highland poet posed the question, 'Who possesses this landscape? The man who bought or inherited it, or I who am possessed by it?' Sunrises and sunsets, trees and mountains, birds and flowers, seas and rivers are there for the poorest as well as the wealthiest to enjoy. The land may not be theirs, but the landscape is.

I used to think a ceilidh was an informal concert where people sang folk songs and tapped their feet to fiddle and bagpipe music. But shortly after going to live in the Highlands, having been invited by a local to drop in one day for a ceilidh, I realised that the essential element of a ceilidh is not in fact music, but armchair conversation. The basic idea is an informal meeting when people share news and ideas, memories and anecdotes. There are few pleasures greater than a ceilidh with friends of long standing, talking into the small hours of the morning. The host will say, 'Let us have another coffee or dram.' Everyone smiles and agrees, not primarily because of the coffee or whisky, but because the conversation and good humour will continue. The variety of topics discussed at a ceilidh are endless – the doings and sayings of saints and sinners, wits and idiots. Long live the ceilidh.

Dean Ramsay in his book *Scottish Reminiscences* tells how in a highland community the ingathering of the harvest had been affected by constant rain. A drying wind was necessary to restore the crops to a fit condition for cutting. One Sunday the minister expressed the needs of his members thus: 'O Lord we pray thee to send us wind; no a rantin', tantin', tearin' wind, but a noohin', soughin', winnin' wind.' There is nothing like being specific! That story reminded me of some villagers who in former times eked out a poor living along the rocky shores of North-West Sutherland. They had a prayer which went, 'We pray Thee Lord, not that wrecks should happen, but that if any wrecks should happen, Thou wilt guide them into our lochs and shores.'

When a farmer who was limping was asked if he had a sore leg, he replied, 'Let me put it this way. I have got one leg that is much better than the other.' Equally memorable was the reply of a bright uncomplaining lady. The day after she had been admitted to hospital for treatment for her arthritis, I asked if she had had a good night's sleep. 'If I was honest I would say "no", but sometimes it is a good thing to have a bad night, for without the occasional bad night, you might not be grateful for the good nights.'

An elderly couple were on a Sunday drive when the husband announced that he had left his glasses at the country hotel where they had stopped for lunch. His wife moaned all the way back to the hotel, telling him he was always forgetting things. As the return journey to the hotel was several miles, she had plenty of time to list all his faults. When they finally pulled up outside the hotel, she said, 'When you are in, could you check if I left my gloves?'

Laughing Matters

My favourite kind of humour is that which appeals to the mind. The greater the incongruity and the more sudden its introduction, the more I enjoy it. I love writers or speakers who play on words, who highlight unexpected humour in everyday happenings, who express in new and memorable ways truths we have long suspected, but have never been able to articulate.

We begin cutting our wisdom teeth the first time we bite off more than we can chew.

Among the runners finishing last in a marathon was an older man wearing a T-shirt that proclaimed: 'The Abominably Slow Man'.

Before the start of a rugby match between Gordonstoun and Inverness Royal Academy, the referee called the two captains together. As he tossed the coin he said to the Gordonstoun captain, Princess Anne's son, 'Tails or Granny?'

When Prince Charles was asked to present the British Press Awards, he began by saying, 'I feel that being here today is rather like asking a pheasant to award prizes to the best shots.'

A visitor to Ayr was having trouble finding the town's popular Alloway Brig O'Doon hotel. He stopped a woman in the street and asked where the Alloway turn-off was. Back came the swift response, 'He's at home in front of the television. I married him 22 years ago.'

Caesar's famous statement might well be revised to describe compulsive shoppers. 'Veni, Vidi, Visa' – 'I came, I saw, I went shopping'.

Interesting definitions:

A diplomat is a man who remembers a lady's birthday but forgets her age.

A gossip columnist is a person with a sense of rumour.

An adult is a person who has stopped growing except in the middle.

A statistician is someone who, if he puts his head in a hot oven and his feet in a bucket of ice water, would remark, 'On average, I feel fine.'

Ulcers are something you get for climbing over molehills.

A wife got so fed up with her husband damaging kitchen utensils by using them for DIY jobs, that one evening she placed a screwdriver and a spanner rather than a knife and fork, at her husband's place at the dinner table. He got the message.

Though divorce is anything but funny, a divorce lawyer's advertisement in a New York train station caused me to smile: 'When diamonds aren't forever'. So also did Rabbi Steinsaltz's definition of a bride as 'a woman who has ceased to search for the ideal man'.

For many years in Perthshire, Dr Heavenor was the minister of St Michael's Church in Crieff. At the same time a Mr Hellier was the minister of a neighbouring church. Not surprisingly Perthshire humorists had a field day.

According to the builder's board, the empty site next to a hospital was earmarked for a new ophthalmic department. Underneath someone had written, 'A site for sore eyes'.

The year Pat Cash defeated the Czech Ivan Lendl in the Australian Open, a spectator hoisted aloft a poster which read, 'Cash is better than a cheque'.

Before symbols replaced words, road signs could be categorised under four headings:

Moralistic ones — Keep right; Go slow

Psychological ones — Hidden Drive

Sensual ones — Soft shoulder

Existentialist ones — Dead end. No Exit

A close friend recently surprised me by asking if I believed in free speech? When I replied that I did, he said, 'Would you make one at our golf club dinner?'

Peter Ustinov got married just before he had to leave for Hollywood to play the part of a slave. At the wedding reception, he joked, 'What impeccable timing'.

When someone sings his own praise, he usually gets the tune too high.

A pessimist's blood type — 'B-negative'.

Shopping for a sports shirt at a department store, a bon vivant found that even the largest size was too tight. 'Where do I go from here?' he asked the saleswoman who was serving him. 'Could I suggest the gym?' she replied.

If animals could talk —

Cows would udder nonsense

Sheep would make baaad jokes

Pigs would talk hogwash

Goats would butt in.

Man does not live by bread alone. He has to handle some hot potatoes, know his onions, and be worth his salt. Little wonder he is often in a stew.

We are told that the right side of our brain controls the left side of our body, and the left side of our brain controls the right side of our body. Are we to conclude from this that left-handed people are the only ones in their right mind?

Tax-collectors and psychologists have this in common. They both believe that no person should keep too much to himself or herself.

The man may think he is the head of the house, but the woman is the neck, and it is the neck that makes the head go the way it wants.

A Glasgow barrister was renowned for two things, his ability in court, and the fact that he was regularly to be seen in the local hotel bars and pubs. One day as he was pleading his client's case in court, he said, 'Judge, let me draw an analogy. It is just as if I saw you going into a pub.' At this stage the judge interrupted him: 'For the sake of accuracy, don't you mean *coming in*?'

Bishop Fulton Sheen told a story about a proud self-righteous man who went to his doctor complaining of a headache. 'Do you occasionally feel a distressing pain in the forehead?' When the man replied that he did, the doctor then asked, 'And do you sometimes feel a throbbing pain in the back of your head, and pressure at the sides?' When the man again answered in the affirmative, the doctor stroked his chin and said, 'I think I know what's wrong. Your halo is too tight.' That was certainly true of little Jack Horner — 'What a good boy am I'. It was true also of the little girl who prayed, 'God bless my Mum, a housewife. God bless my Dad, a policeman. God bless me, one of the best.'

A man who was hoping to move from a rural area to a small town went with an estate agent to look at a house situated in a 'cul-de-sac'. Having been brought up in the country he was unfamiliar with this phrase. As they turned into the cul-de-sac, he said to the agent, 'Where I come from this is called a dead end. What is the difference?' 'About £20,000,' said the estate agent.

A pop star recalled a headmaster telling him he had Van Gogh's ear for music and as much future in show business as Hitler in Israel. Another told how one of the kindest things ever put in her report card was, 'During the last year Rachel has grown older'. Yet another tells how in his rebellious teenage years his headmaster wrote, 'This young man will go far. Just make sure you don't give him a return ticket'.

The comment of a teacher on the report card of a little boy who had no natural gift for singing also made interesting reading,

'Samuel participates very nicely in the group singing by helpful listening.'

Bernard Shaw once received an invitation from a celebrity hunter. The invitation read, 'Lady ——— will be at home on Thursday between four and six'. The playwright returned the card. Underneath he had written, 'Mr Bernard Shaw likewise'.

Richard Baker told of a Promenade Concert when the bass soloist took ill. After due intimation, the orchestra under André Previn carried on. Suddenly just before the soloist spot there appeared on stage a young man, a promenader. André Previn brought him in at the appropriate moment. He sang it right through. The following night the promenaders shouted, 'A promenader has taken ill. Would a soloist take his place?'

A man decided in his thirties to learn the clarinet. For months he produced many strange and unmusical sounds. When he complained one day to a friend that after weeks of practice he still could not play a recognisable tune, his friend said, 'I think you have done very well. After all you started from *screech*.'

In an old book entitled *Abe Lincoln's Yarns and Stories* the author Colonel McClure records one of Lincoln's favourite stories. A minister and a lawyer were travelling by train together. The minister asked the lawyer if he ever made mistakes. 'Very rarely,' the lawyer said, 'but on occasion I must admit I do.' 'And what do you do when you make a mistake?' the minister asked. 'Well, if they are large mistakes, I mend them. If they are small mistakes I let them go. Tell me Reverend, do you ever make mistakes while preaching?' 'Of course,' said the minister. 'And I dispose of them in the same way that you do. Not long ago, for example, I meant to tell the congregation that the devil was the father of liars, but

I made a mistake and said the father of lawyers. But the mistake was so small I let it go!'

For some women counting calories has become a weigh of life.

Nothing depreciates a car faster than having a neighbour buy a new one.

A minister once admitted that life can be pretty grim when you pass eighty, especially if there is a police car behind you.

When a cynic smells flowers, he looks around for the coffin.

There are people to whose good sense you can leave nothing.

Suggested epitaph for a deceased waiter – 'God finally caught his eye.'

I also enjoy unintentional humour.

The confusion of words that sound similar can elicit many a laugh. Some years ago, Grampian Television, which is based in Aberdeen, decided to do a documentary on the magnificent 'sea-eagles' on the island of Rum in the Hebrides. The crossing to the island was so stormy that several of the television crew, including an apprentice, were violently sick. As they were docking in Rum, the young apprentice said to the director, 'Sir, can I ask why we did not just film the "seagulls" in Aberdeen harbour?'

At some time or another most of us are guilty of clangers. I think of a Glasgow couple who were invited by their son's future father-in-law to a meal in a posh restaurant. The host, being a well-to-do vinophile, ordered a top-quality wine. The Glasgow man didn't know much about wine, but he knew what he liked. Taking a deep draught of the fruity red liquid, he said, 'This is lovely. What voltage is it?'

A Sutherland man had been for a body scan to an Edinburgh hospital. Shortly after returning home, a friend called to see how he had got on. 'I am afraid it was not a good report. In fact I have only about six months to live.' Shocked by this news, his friend unthinkingly blurted out. 'Don't worry. It will soon pass.'

A man who was making arrangements for the funeral of his grandfather inquired if it would be possible to have the funeral on the Tuesday. 'I am sorry,' said the undertaker, 'but there have been so many deaths this weekend, that the earliest possible time is Friday.' The grandson had no alternative but to agree to a later date, but as he was leaving he said to the undertaker, 'Would you phone me if you have a cancellation?'

A newly married couple received a gift of an inexpensive but perfectly acceptable tea set. They expressed their gratitude by saying, 'It is just what we need. Up till now we have had to use a good set.'

Noticing a woman about to take a photograph of her husband against the New York skyline, I offered to take one of her and husband. She was delighted. Having taken the picture I asked her if she would like me to take another in case the first did not come out well. 'No, it is all right. You see, I always get double prints.'

Some disc jockeys are long on conversation and short on knowledge. 'And now,' one DJ announced, 'the theme music from *War and Peace* by Leo Tolstoy and his orchestra.'

A man went to his doctor complaining that every time he pressed his neck, he got a shooting pain. The doctor examined his neck but could find nothing wrong. He was baffled until he discovered that the man had two broken fingers.

A man tells how as he was walking home one summer evening, he passed a tent where some small boys were camping. He overheard them talking. 'There is a stone right under my sleeping bag,' said one little voice. Another moaned, 'That is nothing. I'm trying to sleep on a root. I wish I was home in my nice, soft bed.' 'Me too,' cried another. 'I'm cold. Let us go home.' 'Are you crazy?' said the obvious leader of the group. 'If we go home now, our Mums will never let us do this again.'

An airman tells how in their unit there was a rigger named Deeth. Since many pronounced his name Death, he changed it to his mother's maiden name, Morris. Imagine his chagrin when at a later parade he was called forward as Rigger Mortis.

Preaching about the prodigal son, a minister said, 'He looked at the pigs in the trough and thought of home.'

A church bulletin included the following bloomer, 'The Boy Scouts are saving aluminium cans, bottles and other items to be recycled. Proceeds will be used to cripple children.'

When a lady asked the assistant in the bookshop where the self-help books were, the assistant smiled and said, 'Would that not defeat the purpose?'

Robert Dougall, the former BBC newsreader, tells in his autobiography how moved he was by the many letters he received from people living on their own. They wrote to him as a close friend. One dear old lady wrote in a spidery hand to say she was a little deaf. Because of this when he was reading the news, she sat right up close to her 'machine'. 'But,' she added, 'if this puts you off in any way, I will understand and move back.'

The actor Michael Crawford tells how as he was once shopping in an English supermarket, a lady approached him. 'Has anyone ever told you that you look like Michael Crawford?' When he replied in the affirmative, she nudged him and said, 'I bet you wish you had his kind of money.'

When a salesman asked the receptionist, 'Are you sure your boss is not in his office?' she replied, 'Are you doubting his word?'

In a pep talk to one class about working harder, the headmaster said, 'In the next exam I want you all to be above the class average.'

In an essay on the poet John Milton, a pupil wrote, 'Milton wrote "Paradise Lost". Then his wife died and he wrote "Paradise Regained".'

A father tells how early one March his youngest child came home from school in tears. When asked what was wrong, he said, 'I have just learned to spell February and now it is gone.'

'Ethics are vital to the successful businessman,' said a man to his friend. 'To give you an example — an old customer paid his bill today with a £20 note. As he was leaving, I discovered that he had mistakenly handed me two £20 notes stuck together. Immediately the question of ethics arose. Should I tell my partner?'

A crusty duchess who persistently borrowed other people's chauffeurs demanded to be collected from Claridge's. Getting into the car she asked the driver what his name was. 'James,' he said, only to be told she never addressed a chauffeur by his Christian name. 'What's your surname?' she went on. 'Darling,' came the reply. She blushed and said: 'Drive on, James.'

The *Daily Mail* quoted a divorce hearing where the husband said, 'When I am in a temper I am liable to throw things at my wife, but I always aim to miss. This time she moved with unfortunate consequences.'

The postwar Cabinet Minister George Brown was once standing at a reception in South America, next to a person wearing the most beautiful purple gown. As was not uncommon, George was somewhat the worse for drink. When the music started up he asked the magnificently clad figure for a dance. His invitation was declined, the person curtly pointing out that it was the national anthem that was being played, and that he was in fact the Papal Nuncio.

Family Matters

When Harry Truman became President on the death of Roosevelt the press flocked to the farm in which he had been brought up. One of the reporters said to his mother, 'You must feel very proud of your son Harry, President of the United States.' 'Yes,' she said, 'I am very proud of Harry, but I have another son out ploughing the fields and I am just as proud of him.' What a wise mother.

I once watched children play a game of musical chairs. When the music stopped it resembled a rugby scrum. The competition was fierce until there were only two left – a little boy and a really good-looking wee girl. At this stage I got the feeling that the little boy, who had previously pushed and shoved, let the little girl win. I also got the feeling he fancied her!

The 18th-century Georgian House in which we lived for a year in Charlotte Square in Edinburgh had some valuable artifacts and paintings. Shortly after our arrival we were shown a copy of a document which had been recently given to the local Fire Brigade. It listed the most valuable things in the house. The idea was that if there was ever a fire, the listed items would be rescued first. When I observed that my wife and I did not appear on the list, I was reminded of the question posed by the Chief Rabbi Jonathan Sacks in his Reith lectures. He asked his listeners to imagine they were standing in a City Art Gallery. Suddenly a fire breaks out and spreads with enormous speed. In front of them is a priceless painting by Leonardo da Vinci. To their right is one of the country's most respected elder statesmen. To their left is their 4-year-old daughter. You can only rescue one. Which do you save? A few might argue that if we rushed out into the open air carrying the painting or accompanying the elder statesman, we might have contributed to the country's greater good. 'But,' asks Jonathan Sacks, 'would anyone thereafter ever again trust us as a human being?'

An army is invading our country. It is going to capture and take possession of everything we have, every political office, business, school, college and council. Nothing will be left to us. This army is composed of the babies and youngsters in our homes. They are the future citizens, the future teachers, directors, politicians. What happens to them, the kind of people they will become, will determine the quality of life in this country twenty–thirty years from now. No task is therefore more important than the education and training of these children in honesty, self-discipline, generosity, love and forgiveness.

In Aultbea in Wester Ross an experiment was once tried in which young offenders shared a camp with children with mental handicaps. One day the physically strong helped the mentally retarded climb a nearby hill. On arriving back at camp, a youngster who suffered from Down Syndrome put his arms round the older lad, who had accompanied him up the hill and had shared his lunch with him, and said, 'I love you.' The young offender burst into tears. Later the camp leader discovered that no one had ever before said that to him. Many factors contribute to and shape the final personality of young people. But of these caring love is by far the most important. If children are not loved during their growing years, they are more likely to become unlovely and unhappy adults.

Shortly after the end of the Second World War a couple adopted a Polish baby. Several months later, the mother wrote to the education authorities asking where she could take evening classes in Polish, as she wanted to be able to understand her little one when he started to speak! We smile at that, knowing that the language and the accent of the child will be that of the parents, but what parents often fail to realise is that the values and faith and outlook of the growing child will also to a marked extent be that of the parents. Children are natural mimics. They act like their parents in spite of all the efforts to teach them good manners.

Tell your child to lie for you and he will learn to lie to you.

A man tells how on an aeroplane journey, he sat beside an affable stranger. The stranger was travelling with his wife to their daughter's wedding. On hearing this, the man offered his congratulations. The stranger gave a wry laugh. 'Actually this is her third marriage, and she is still in her twenties. It is a funny feeling to be going to such a wedding.' Periodic doses of intimacy are no substitute for an enduring relationship in which there is warmth, companionship and joy. Those who live by a philosophy of touch and go, miss so much. When children are involved the emotional and social costs are great.

Dr James Weatherhead tells how he once talked to some school children about the unique Moderatorial clothes. He explained that what he was wearing was what people wore in the 16th century when they went to the royal court. Dr Weatherhead later regretted not having worded it differently, for one little boy, with a sad face, said, 'My Mummy and Daddy are going to court to see who is going to look after me.' A report, 'Torn Lives', which looks at the effect of the breakup of relationships, not on the couple, but on the children, does not make happy reading.

The headmaster of a remand school for boys in Glasgow once told me how the parents were supposed to visit the boys regularly. The staff had noticed that one boy had received no parental visits. Nor did he receive any letters from home. So the headmaster told the boy to write his parents and say that the headmaster would like to see them. When the mother finally came, he asked why she or her husband never visited Johnnie. Her reply shook him. 'You know, when Johnnie's letter arrived, I wondered at first who it was from. I did not recognise the writing. But then my daughter said, "It is probably from Johnnie." And sure enough it was. You know, it is a case of out of sight, out of mind.'

A prominent businessman once spoke to a colleague about his son's behaviour. The colleague thought he was going to hear the usual story about the irresponsibility of young people. But in fact the man said with considerable sadness that he had been so caught up in the business and social whirl, that he had spent very little time with his son. Not surprisingly they had become strangers. It seems to have been similar with the writer of that strange Old Testament book, *The Song of Solomon*. He laments, 'They made me keeper of the vineyards, but my own vineyard I have not kept.' It is a humbling fact that many of the big names in the Bible did not rate very highly as parents. Isaac made the elementary error of having favourites, preferring Esau to Jacob. Jacob did not learn from experience. He proceeded to make the same mistake with Joseph and in doing so put the rest of the family's back up. Eli the priest helped the boy Samuel on the road to righteousness, but he could not control his own sons. And when Samuel in his time grew to be a great man, busy with the affairs of God, it is recorded that his sons were intent on their own profit. They took bribes and perverted the course of justice.

I recall a teenager saying, 'When I asked Dad if we could do something, he always used to say, "Oh, we'll see." I soon learned he really meant, "No".' To be a parent is to be more than a provider of food, clothing and pocket-money. Making time to help a child build that Lego truck, or draw that Humpty Dumpty, or share in a game, can pay handsome dividends. Our children need our presence more than our presents. Our work will wait while we show our child the rainbow, but the rainbow won't wait while we do our work.

A little girl had worked hard at school making a surprise present for her parents. She had moulded the clay dish, fired it and painted it. She was justifiably proud of it. But as she rushed into her home with it, she tripped and fell. The dish broke with a fearful ceramic crash. Hearing her screams, her parents rushed through from the lounge. Her father seeing what had happened unthinkingly said, 'It does not really matter, dear.' Fortunately her mother was much wiser. Taking the little girl in her arms, she hugged her and said, 'It does matter, dear. It matters a very great deal.' Is there anything more demoralising than the feeling that what we do does not matter?

It does not take a car to run us down. Sometimes as a result of environment or a very critical parent, or humiliation suffered at school, people start running themselves down. The effects of self-deprecation can be long-term, and can take longer to heal than cracked bones.

While on holiday in Scotland, a young couple with a 4-year-old son stayed overnight at a Highland farm. During breakfast the farmer was called away to attend to a ewe which was having trouble lambing. The family followed and watched with great interest the farmer deliver the lamb. When he gave it a hard slap, it took its first breath and bleated loudly. The little boy who had been closely watching the proceedings finally spoke up, 'Oh you daft wee thing, that'll learn you not to go in there again.'

A little white boy brought home a little black classmate to play. Introducing him to his Mum, he said, 'Me and Jackson are exactly the same age, only he is different. He is left-handed.'

Preparing a little girl for confirmation, the priest asked her, 'What is the first and most important sacrament?' 'Marriage,' was the prompt response. 'No,' said the priest. 'Baptism is the first and most important sacrament.' 'Not in our family,' said the little girl haughtily. 'We are respectable.'

It is admirable for a man to take his son fishing or golfing, but I would not be surprised if there is a special place in heaven for the father who takes his daughter shopping.

After the birth of twins, one mother had four children under three years of age. Her e-mails to her sister became shorter and shorter. One day when winter was in full swing, her sister received an e-mail. All it said was: '4 kids, 4 colds, 4 lorn'.

In one of her books Lorraine Collins offered a suggestion as how to get children to tidy up their rooms. 'Don't be negative or nagging. Encourage the child in a positive manner, by finding something about the room you like, and praising him for it sincerely. Say for instance, "You certainly do keep your ceiling neat!"'

The anthropologist Gregory Bateson tells the story of a little boy he knew who asked his father, 'Do fathers always know more than their sons?' 'Yes,' the father told him. The boy's next question was, 'Who invented the steam engine?' 'James Watt,' said his father. 'Well, why didn't James Watt's father invent it?'

Lord Macfarlane of Bearsden tells how when one of his daughters was young, she had one day misbehaved so badly that she was finally sent to bed. An hour later he went to see her. 'I sat on her bed and took the moral high ground. I explained rather pompously that her conduct was unacceptable, that she was letting the family down. Her behaviour would not be tolerated. It had to improve...' When he had finished his stern lecture, he asked her if she had anything to say. 'Daddy, do you know that the hairs from your moustache go up your nose?'

A father, who was listening to his young son's evening prayers, was startled to hear him say, 'God if you can't make me a better boy, don't worry. I am having a good time.'

A preacher tells how his 8-year-old son one night came into the living room and said, 'I am going to bed. I am going to be praying. Does anybody want anything?' Unfortunately prayer for many is an Aladdin's lamp, not a time of quiet communion with God.

Little Elsie and her aunt were at the art gallery. Standing before a large painting of the early Christians being thrown to the lions, Elsie suddenly burst into tears. Trying to comfort her, her aunt said, 'It is sad, isn't it?' 'Yes,' said Elsie, 'That little lion is not getting any.'

When a boy was asked one day by his parents how it was that in exams, he came consistently lower than his friend, the lad replied, 'Ogilvy has clever parents.'

As a mother was tucking her little girl into bed, her daughter gazed intently at her and said solemnly, 'You know, Mum, I would risk my life for you.' The mother gave her a big hug and said, 'You know what, Eliza, I would risk my life for you too.' There was a moment of silence while each digested the other's pledges. 'Mum,' said Eliza, 'I have just one question, what does "risk" mean?'

When asked to get a can of soup out of the pantry cupboard, a 5-year-old refused, saying it was dark and scary in there. The mother explained that God is everywhere and would protect her. Dutifully the little girl went to the pantry, stuck her head just inside and said, 'God, would you please hand me a can of chicken soup?'

A 10-year-old was visiting a cemetery with his mother. As they walked down the rows of graves, he read a few of the glowing epitaphs on the head-stones. 'Mum,' he asked, 'Where do they bury the naughty people?' A father had an equally disconcerting experience. As he and his son were walking in the woods, they came across a dead bird. 'What happened?' asked the boy. When his Dad replied that the bird had died and gone to heaven, the lad thought for a moment and then asked, 'Did God throw him back?'

Children's theological questions are sometimes even more disturbing than their behaviour. Many parents and grandparents can recall exchanging half-pleading, half-terrified glances with their spouse, each hoping the other had some kind of meaningful answer to questions like: 'Is God a man or woman?'; 'What clothes does God wear?'; 'How can God hear everything when so many are praying at the one time?'; 'Why did God create insects?'; 'How far away is heaven?'; 'How long has God been alive?'; 'Who made God?'

Perhaps because children do not think in abstract terms, they have an uncanny way of reducing the mysterious and inexplicable to their own terms. Describing how God creates people, one boy wrote, 'He first draws us, then cuts us out.' Another said, 'God flies around in the sky. Sometimes he stops behind a cloud to have something to eat. He goes down to land at night to see shepherds and talk to them.' As well as interpreting Biblical metaphors and word pictures literally, children equate unfamiliar words and phrases with ones they understand. 'Harold be thy name... Lead us not into Thames station.' Both were attempts to understand what was confusing.

'Will there be sweets in heaven?' Like the other questions quoted earlier, that is not an easy question to answer. To say there won't be any sweets in heaven, could give children the impression that heaven is a most unattractive place. Though one might be tempted to say there will be the best kind of sweets in heaven, I think I would prefer simply to say, 'I don't know, but I am sure heaven will be a very happy place.' Children have to learn there are many questions about God and heaven to which we don't know the answer. Many and varied are the attributes parents and Sunday school teachers need, but one that is not required is the ability to answer every question a child asks. Children don't think the less of us for saying we don't know. When religious questions have threatened to drown me in a sea of philosophy, I am sometimes tempted to quote a former President of Harvard University, 'I don't know much about God, but what I do know has changed my life.'

Have you ever asked yourself why we smile when we see a baby? Is it because we see someone without any defensive layers, someone whose smile we know to be fully genuine and without guile?

A small child is someone who can wash his hands without getting the soap wet.

The four words 'We cannot afford it' should be part of every child's education. A child who has never heard these words has been cheated by his parents.

Youth is a time of rapid change. While our children are between 12 and 17, parents can age 30 years.

I warm to the remark of the man who said that watching his sons grow up had been a learning experience: 'I saw in them my own faults and my wife's virtues.'

In the fantasy world portrayed by Walt Disney's box office successes, *The Little Mermaid, Beauty and the Beast, Robin Hood* and *Aladdin*, no mention is made of the mothers of Ariel, Belle, Maid Marion or Jasmin, only their fathers. How often in the real world we continue to underestimate the importance of mothers.

A little boy was listening to his grandfather relate stories of his time as a soldier in the Gordon Highlanders. 'I fought in Africa, in Italy and Germany. I fought with Montgomery, I fought with Wavell, and I fought with Alexander.' The wee lad, more than slightly puzzled by what he had heard, said, 'Grandad, could you not get on with anyone?'

Another small boy said to his grandfather, 'If you are happy, why don't you tell your face?'

Some men are like the father whose 4-year-old daughter asked, 'Daddy, are you afraid of cows?' When he informed her that he was not, she asked if he was afraid of spiders. When he again informed her that he wasn't, she then asked, 'Daddy, are you not afraid of anything but Mum?'

Food for Thought

A psychiatrist once asked a man who had attempted to take his own life, 'What part of you did you want to kill?' A good question. Are there parts of us we would like to bury? Are there elements in us we recognise and repudiate and long to be rid of? Are there painful memories and regrets we long to lay to rest?

A friendly postman paused to chat with a 4-year-old about his baby sister. 'Can she talk?' the postman asked. 'No,' said the little fellow, 'she has a few teeth but her words have not come in yet.' It is a great day when words do come in, for it is through words that we can share our thoughts and feelings with others. Words are the beginning of everything, of understanding, of relationships. For good or ill most things are started by words. No modern tool or invention is as magical, mysterious or powerful as words. What power they have to make us laugh or cry, to break hearts or help heal them, to put a lilt in our step or give us sleepless nights, to stir up hatred or bring about reforms.

A ticket inspector tells of an incident which happened on a train bound for London. In a first class compartment he saw an elderly gentleman who, he strongly suspected from the way he was dressed, was not a first class traveller. When asked for his ticket, the old man fumbled in his pocket, but could not find it. After waiting patiently for some time, the inspector finally told the man he would return in five minutes. Instead of checking the other tickets, he stood at the end of the corridor, certain that at the next station, the man would make a hurried exit. But not so. When approached again, the man, full of apologies and to the inspector's surprise, produced the necessary first class ticket. On arrival at Euston, the inspector spotted him on the platform beckoning to a porter to help him with his luggage. When half-way towards him, the porter suddenly noticed a well-dressed lady stepping off the train. Quickly changing direction, he took her case. Seeing this happen, and being ashamed of misjudging the old man, the inspector volunteered to carry his cases. At the taxi-rank the old man took out his wallet and gave the inspector five pounds, saying, 'Do me a favour. If you meet that porter will you tell him what I have given you for carrying my cases, and tell him never to judge a sausage by its skin.' Later that day the inspector did meet the porter and told him what had happened. 'Well,' said the porter, 'should you ever meet that old man again, tell him that the well-dressed lady whose case I carried is blind. She is a regular traveller, and whenever I am free, I help her, and never take a penny for it. Tell him to apply his own words to himself.'

An elderly lady who travelled a great deal, made a point of learning the word for beautiful in the language of the countries she was to visit – *beau, bello, schön, hermoso*, or *boyoch*... The reason was that she wanted to be able to pay a compliment. It is amazing what a compliment does for the sense of hearing! We all have a sweet tooth for a word of praise. It saddens me when people give up paying compliments, for when they give up saying what is charming, they very often give up thinking what is charming.

The American columnist Art Buchwald once wrote about a man who single-handedly tried to reform New York city. They were travelling together in a taxi-cab. When they got to their destination, Buchwald's friend paid the driver and said, 'Thanks for the ride. You did a superb job driving.' The driver was obviously surprised by this unexpected compliment, but thanked him for it. When Buchwald later asked his friend what had prompted the compliment, he said, 'I was just trying to bring back love into New York City.' He then went on to explain, 'Suppose that taxi-driver has twenty more fares today. That means that because I was nice to him, he is more likely to be nice to twenty other people. And these people in turn are going to be nicer to waiters, customers, employees, and maybe even their own families.' When a sceptical Buchwald asked if it worked, his friend replied, 'I think so, and anyway nothing is lost if it does not.'

After reading an article about the world's greatest verbal put-downs, I was tempted to write a similar article about some of the world's great compliments. One I would certainly include concerns the German composer Brahms. He was a close friend of Johann Strauss who wrote the 'Blue Danube' and many other glorious melodies. Once when they met in Vienna, Strauss asked Brahms if he would honour him by signing his autograph book. On a blank page in the book Brahms quickly wrote the music for the opening bars of the Blue Danube. Then he wrote underneath, 'Unfortunately not by Brahms!' The wonderful thing about compliments is that they enrich the lives of those who receive them without impoverishing those who write or voice them.

Abraham Lincoln in his day was hated by half the American nation and misunderstood by the other half. To an old black lady who one day thanked him for what he was trying to do for her people, he said, 'You have given a cup of cold water to a very thirsty man.' Though the words of Brahms and that old lady were written and spoken in a few seconds, the memory of them lasted a lifetime. One more thought about compliments. Nobody needs them quite as much as those who have stopped complimenting others.

The Spanish philosopher Salvador de Mariaga once remarked 'The person who is nothing but, is not even.' By that he meant that the nurse or doctor who can only speak about medicine and hospital life is not even a good nurse or doctor; that the lawyer, teacher or clergyman who has no wider interests than law or teaching or the church, is not even a good lawyer, teacher or minister. John Arlott applied this criterion to cricket commentators. 'What do they know of cricket who only cricket know?' The dangers of specialisation are well illustrated by a story about a former Latin professor. When he retired after teaching for fifty years, his colleagues gave him a gold watch (with Roman numerals on it), and a hearty round of applause. In his reply he said, 'I owe my success to specialisation. I chose Latin and stayed with it. I have only one regret. I should have stayed with the dative and left the ablative alone.' How different it was with a former Italian professor at Glasgow University. In addition to delivering his university lectures, Professor Meiklejohn found time to write a weekly ornithology column for the *Glasgow Herald*. His wider interests made him a much more interesting personality.

The Duke of Buckingham was a powerful figure in England in the 17th century. One historian says of him, 'He was once a headliner, now he has shrunk to a footnote.' That verdict applies to many notables other than the Duke of Buckingham. History has a habit of shrinking to mere footnotes those whose greatness depends only on worldly prestige, position, power or property. I remember once glancing through an old history book entitled, *Significant Events in British and European History*. I discovered that St Francis lived during the reign of the Emperor Frederick. The book mentioned no other significant contemporary to the 'insignificant' monk who devoted his life to helping the poor and the lepers, and I have the suspicion Frederick was mentioned only because he died 1250. Few of us know what the war in Crimea was all about, or who the opposing generals were, but we all know of a young woman with a lantern in her hand walking among the beds of wounded soldiers. It is strange that Florence Nightingale rather than the generals should be remembered, or again is it? History has a habit of righting things in the long run. God seems to run his universe on the basis that only greatness based on service will last. Jesus said, 'He who would be great among you, let him become the servant of all.' True aristocracy lies not in genealogy, or fame or wealth, but in service and usefulness.

I cannot understand why people consult astrologers with their charts, or card readers shuffling the tools of their trade. To remove the secret from the unknown future would be to remove much of the joy from the present. A Futuroid camera would be an appalling invention. How much more exciting is a live television broadcast of a football match to a tele-recording where you already know the result. I am glad that we move into each new day as we row a boat, our faces towards the wake rather than the prow. I am glad that though the past is lighted by memory, the future is veiled, that as the wise writer of Proverbs said long ago, 'the glory of God is to keep things hidden'.

Life experiences can produce a softening of judgments. Fixed opinions about life can sometimes become unfixed when the plight or experience of a loved one weighs upon our sympathies. A Dr Ernest Campbell gives some examples from his own experience.

I think of a couple who were very outspoken against young people living together until their daughter started to share space with a live-in boyfriend whom they liked.

I think of a woman who regarded Aids as a divine judgment until her son tested HIV positive.

I think of a man who was bitter and vocal against homosexuals until his own son came out of the closet.

I think of a woman who was very anti-Japanese until her unemployed husband came home waving a generous managerial job offer from Nissan.

I think of a doctor to whom a drunk was a drunk until his brother told him that he was about to enter a recovery programme for alcoholics.

Seldom in life do we regret being too merciful in our judgments of others.

'I never fly in small private planes,' said George Burns. 'If I am going down I want to have an audience with me.' George Burns was joking, but unfortunately there are people in every sphere of life who always crave an audience. What a strain they put on their physical and nervous systems.

'Stop worrying about your own halo and shine up your neighbour's.' That is probably as good a prescription for getting on with people as I know. It shifts the emphasis from self to others. How often people respond to the image we give them of themselves. The basic problem with many partnerships is that they have stopped shining up each other's halo. 'My wife only knows how to find fault.' 'My husband seldom thanks or compliments me.' Shining up someone's halo can set the heart singing.

The motto of Belfast, 'Pro tanto quid retribuamus', does not mean, '*How much can you get for a quid?*', but 'In return for so much what shall we give?' I was brought up to have a fear of debt. My father would quote words which I later discovered were first spoken by the Apostle Paul, 'Owe no man anything.' Though there are dangers in going into the red financially, in many other respects we will always be in the red. In fact a good measure of people's maturity is their awareness of how indebted they are. Not even the largest ledger in the world could contain all the things by which our lives have been enriched and for which we could never possibly pay. Innumerable are the little-known people who have contributed to the quality of life we enjoy.

Beside the cable-car station in the Swiss village of Château d'Oex was a notice printed in three languages. In English it said, 'Please do not pick flowers'. In German it said, 'It is forbidden to pick the flowers'. In French it said, 'Those who love the mountains leave them their flowers'. In so many spheres of life, the French approach is the best. On the outskirts of an English town there was an area of ground which had become a fearful eyesore. Many of the residents had written angry letters to the local council telling them that something would have to be done about it. But nothing was done. One man however tried a different approach. Having taken a picture of the eyesore, he then drew a plan showing how at minimum cost it could be landscaped. He also painted a picture of how it would finally look with shrubs and flowers. He even got estimates for the cost of the work. Within a week of sending the plans and estimates to the Council, he received back a delightful letter thanking him for drawing their attention to the eyesore and promising that the work of improving the site would be started as soon as possible.

We have all got three ages – a chronological age determined by the calendar, a biological age programmed to our genes, and a psychological age programmed to our outlook. What is abundantly clear is that our psychological age affects our biological age. How often the human spirit becomes jaded before the body. If we become self-centred or lose the stimulus of being of use, we will be tobogganed into ripe old age before we are fifty. The beauty consultant Helena Rubenstein was well aware of this. She said, 'I have never had my face lifted. I prefer to have my spirits lifted.'

Have you ever thought what the world would be like —

if we really worked to see that others were as well off as we are? All we would have to fight about would be who could be the most generous.

Have you ever thought what the world would be like —

if we took pleasure each day in what we could do for others, rather than in what we have done or gained for ourselves? Many of our worries, jealousies and resentments would disappear. By the end of the year our world would be much larger and our troubles fewer.

Has it ever struck you?

that some people so treasure the truth that they use it with great economy

that success is relative — the more success, the more relatives

that good habits are so much easier to get out of than bad ones

that when people manage to break a bad habit, they often have the pieces mounted and framed.

I will forgive a person a great deal if he or she has enthusiasm. Enthusiasm is one of life's most attractive qualities. Enthusiasm is a sparkle in the eye, a skip in the step, a surge of energy to execute dreams. Enthusiasts are fighters. They have staying qualities.

Why do we talk of reporters 'covering' parliamentary or rural affairs? It is the politicians who seem determined to cover things up. Journalists spend most of their life uncovering them, and the other half enduring reprisals from powerful politicians for doing so.

One evening the artist William Hunt taught a class by the lakeside. He noticed one of his students spending a great deal of time painting an old barn. He had not even begun to paint the glories of the evening sky. 'Son,' said the wise teacher, 'It won't be light for long. You have to choose between shingles and sunsets. There is time for only one or the other.' Probably life's commonest failure is the crowding out of things that really matter by things that do not matter all that much.

A business director had a standard question he asked those he interviewed. From their answer, he felt he could deduce a great deal about the applicant. The question was, 'If someone gave you ten thousand pounds, what would be the first thing you would do?' To the director's surprise, but delight, one young lad, instead of saying he would buy a car, or take his girl-friend for a luxury holiday, said, 'I would write and say "Thank you".'

In Robert Bolt's *A Man for all Seasons*, Richard, a young Cambridge Scholar, approaches Sir Thomas More for some vocational advice. Richard is ambitious, anxious to rise in the world. He is nonplussed when More suggests, 'Why not be a teacher? You would be a fine teacher, perhaps even a great one.' Richard contemptuously retorts, 'And if I was, who would know?' Sir Thomas replies, 'You, your pupils, your friends, God. Not a bad public that.' Not bad at all!

The Adam and Eve story, with Adam blaming Eve and Eve blaming the serpent, is as modern as the morning newspaper. A university professor said he sometimes wondered if an MA degree stood for Master of Alibis. Recognition of our own guilt being about the most acute agony we can know, the temptation is strong to garnish our own traits and tarnish other people's. A display of bad temper in others is righteous indignation with us. Other people's longing for revenge is a desire for justice on our part. The dubious business practice of our competitors is business acumen with us.

> *Stubborness we deprecate*
> *But firmness we condone;*
> *The former is our neighbour's trait*
> *The latter is our own.*

A tearful wife once said, 'It is not so much what my husband says, it is the way he shouts at me.' An office secretary said, 'My boss takes everything I do for granted.' A harassed parent said, 'All we get from our teenage son is surliness.' For lack of courtesy and good manners, many a working day is ruined, many a friendship wrecked and many a home broken. Good manners are an essential lubricant of human nature. Words like 'please' and 'thank you' change demands into requests. They prevent strained relationships generating excessive heat. They are an indication that other people are our equals. Courtesy is like the zero in arithmetic. By itself it may appear of little value, but what value it adds to everything else. If I was allowed to add a beatitude, it could well be 'Blessed are the courteous'.

To a toad, beauty is popeyes, a yellow belly and spotted beak.

A wise man was once asked, 'Why is it that you tell everybody who wants to become your disciple to look into this pond and tell you what he sees?' 'That is very simple,' said the teacher. 'I am ready to accept those who tell me they see the fish swimming around. But I have no use for those who see only their own image in the water, those who are in love with their ego.' I was reminded of that on hearing a woman say of her partner with whom she had just split, 'We had a lot in common. We loved the same person – HIM.' An author, who was proudly extolling his many virtues and achievements, paused momentarily: 'But enough of talking about myself. Let us talk about you. What do you think of my latest book?'

In a fit of deep depression, a man wrote to Rabbi Menachem Mendel Schneerson. 'I would like your help. I wake up each day sad and apprehensive. I cannot concentrate. I find it hard to pray. I keep the commandments but I find no spiritual satisfaction. I go to the synagogue but I feel alone. I begin to wonder what life is about.' Instead of writing a reply, the Rabbi circled the first word of every sentence and returned the letter. The ringed word was 'I'. The Rabbi knew that mental health and happiness live in a realm, 'Not-I'.

Charles Dickens tells us it was similar with Mr Dombey. *'Dombey and Son. These three words conveyed the one idea of Mr Dombey's life. The earth was made for Dombey and Son to trade in, and the sun and the moon were made to give them light. Rivers and seas were formed to float their ships; rainbows gave them promise of fair weather; winds blew for or against their enterprise; stars and planets circled in their orbits to preserve inviolate a system of which they were the centre... AD had no concern with Anno Domini, but stood for Anno Dombey and Son.'* Too many of us like Mr Dombey suffer from I-strain, from an overgrown love of self. In our writing and speaking our 'I's are too close together. When we converse with other egotists, it is an 'I' for an 'I'. How often we are guilty of thinking more about what we intend to say than what is being said to us. We long for the other person to stop talking so that we can relate our misfortunes which are so much worse, or our adventures which of course are more interesting.

> *How very self-centred some people can be.*
> *They think of themselves instead of me!*

People who are always me-deep in conversation are not attractive or happy people. One of the most important discoveries anyone can make is that there are other people in the world beside themselves.

You cannot say the Lord's prayer, and ever once say I
You cannot say the Lord's prayer and ever once say my
You cannot say the Lord's prayer and not pray for another
For when you ask for daily bread, you must include your brother
For others are included in each and every plea
From the beginning to the end of it, it does not once say me

A New York minister Maurice Boyd developed the same theme. 'If you put self at the centre, you had better be prepared to find your outer limits there; and that can be very lonely. If you believe only in justice, and not in mercy, you'd better not make any mistakes. If you are a gossip, don't look for any confidences. If you believe that life is a rat race, you must not hope to find any dignity in it. If your basic stance is confrontation, don't expect people to knock on your door when what they need is tenderness. If you are ruthless on the way up, you shouldn't look for sympathy on the way down. If you never forgive, you must never offend. If what you are after is security, you'd better forget about ecstasy. If your work is your life, you had better keep one eye on your relationships.'

Life is to be enjoyed. It is not a rehearsal, even though some people seem not to have got their act together. At the end of his life Malcolm Muggeridge, the former Editor of *Punch*, confessed that what troubled him most as he looked back on his life were not sins of commission or omission, but that he had often picked the third-rate instead of the first-rate, and had gone after the worst when he could have had the best. He had chosen cardboard shoes when he might have had leather; processed cheese when he could have had cheddar; artificial flowers when the primroses were out.

It was said of a Dr Hugo Turner that he 'so wanted to be all things to all people that Turner was not only the proper but the inevitable name for him. The corkscrew shaped his course.' How different it was with Lord Soper, the Methodist preacher and Labour peer. At his memorial service in Westminster Abbey, Tony Benn said, 'Donald Soper was wholly committed to the cause of peace and social justice. He said what he believed and believed what he said. In a world of weathercocks whirling in the wind of fashion, he was a signpost.' So was Edward Everett, the president of Harvard University in the mid-19th century. When a storm arose over the proposed admission of a black student to the University, Everett made his position clear: 'If this young man passes the entrance examination, he will be admitted, and if the white students choose to withdraw, all the income of the college will be devoted to his education.'

A doctor tells of a man who had fallen and cracked his head on the hard cement. The result was that he lost all sense of colour. Thereafter he saw everything in terms of black, white and grey. A world without colour – what a loss that would be. Would Wordsworth have put pen to paper had he come across a host of grey daffodils, fluttering and dancing in the breeze?

'Time is money' goes the old adage. But whose time and whose money? Is one person's wasted time intrinsically more valuable than another's? This question often surfaces. Many repair firms quote an hourly rate. They also promise they will arrive 'first thing in the morning', or 'early afternoon'. Both tend however to be moveable feasts. The firms concerned do not seem to worry how much it may be costing their client to sit at home, waiting, waiting... The message seems to be that there is nothing so precious as one's own time, but nothing so expendable as someone else's.

Victor Reisel, an American journalist, spoke out strongly against the power of the Mafia in New York City. For doing so he paid an awful price, acid being thrown into his face, permanently blinding him. Months later he wrote, 'My great struggle has not been with blindness, but against hate and a longing for vengeance. But fortunately I finally realised that hate would corrode me more than any acid. I may have been deprived of my sight, but no one is going to deprive me of my peace of mind.'

A man who translated the Bible into the language of a remote New Guinea tribe, tells how he struggled with how best to communicate the idea of forgiveness. Finally he chose the phrase, 'God does not hang up jawbones against us.' This unusual phrase was based on a longstanding New Guinea custom. When a tribesman was murdered, his jawbone was removed and hung over the door of one of his relatives. It hung there until revenge had been exacted. But when Christianity came to that part of the world the tribes took down the jawbones. Having learned that God does not hang up jawbones against them, they were more willing to forgive those who wronged them.

In Loch Leven there is a small island with a Gaelic name which translated means, 'Isle of Discussion'. People who had quarrelled were taken to the island with a minimal amount of food and water. They were not allowed off until they had settled their difference. How often I have wished there was such an island nearby to which I could have sent people who no longer speak.

My grandson Liam has a night-light in the form of a Noah's Ark. The light shines through pictures of Noah and his wife, two dogs, two elephants, two giraffes and two grizzly bears. Like other children he loves singing about how the animals went into the Ark two by two. I personally find Isaiah's magnificent picture of the animal kingdom a far more moving one. It is a picture of longstanding enemies living happily together, of a community where there is no more hurt.

Then the wolf shall live with the sheep and the leopard lie down with the kid; the calf and the young lion shall grow together, and a little child shall lead them; the cow and the bear shall be friends, and their young shall lie down together. The lion shall eat straw like cattle; the infant shall play over the hole of the cobra, and the young child dance over the viper's nest. They shall not hurt or destroy...

How I wish toymakers had made Isaiah's zoos as well as Noah's Arks.

What a debt modern astronomy owes to Copernicus and Galileo for having the courage to voice their doubts about the astronomical beliefs of their day. Likewise one of the greatest advances in medicine resulted from Lord Lister doubting contemporary medical beliefs concerning wound infection. When Einstein was asked what led him to the theory of relativity, he replied, 'I challenged an axiom.' He doubted whether Newton's laws explained all the facts. What many forget is that the high peaks of Biblical religion were also scaled by people who had the courage to examine accepted beliefs with an open mind. Job called into question the religious theories of his day concerning suffering. He uttered some of the most hopeless sounds a man has ever uttered, as well as some of the most triumphant affirmations of trust in God. 'I know that my redeemer liveth.' Micah doubted the worthwhileness of many of the religious practices of his day, the sacrificial slaughtering of thousands of animals, the pouring out of what he called 'rivers of holy oil'. Habbakuk doubted the justice of God. Such honest reflection led Job and Micah and Habbakuk to maturer faith, which they in turn passed on to others. What a debt we owe to those in the past who had the courage to doubt some of the scientific and religious beliefs of their day.

Many think of leisure as freedom from work and other responsibilities. Others think of leisure as 'getting away from it all'. Yet others as 'taking it easy'. The logical conclusion of these definitions is that the highest form of leisure would be death. For many of our ancestors there was precious little free time, virtually no getting away from it all or any opportunity to take it easy. I like to think of leisure as the flowering of a free spirit, rather than the filling of free time, as a means of getting it together with oneself, family and friends, rather than a means of getting away from it all. Perhaps the major distinction between what we call work and what we call leisure, is that in our free time, however active we might still be, we make our own choices and our own decisions. Leisure is an opportunity for creativity, renewal and reflection, an opportunity to rediscover the wholeness of living, to gain perspective. In the face of so many interesting challenges and social interests, and voluntary organisations crying out for help, it is much more enriching to take life on, than to take it easy.

Professor Tom Driver, one of my teachers in New York, contracted neck cancer shortly after recovering from heart surgery. A close friend said to him one day that his story was becoming more and more like that of Job. 'Perhaps,' he said, 'but I have far better friends.'

Followers of athletics have learned to appreciate the track and field concept of personal best. Often after a race the commentator will say, 'Olwen Jones' time is a personal best.' The audience cheers. Olwen may not have been the race winner. She might have come in third, but the spectators are delighted to learn her time was the best she had ever done. Perhaps the idea of 'personal best' should have a larger place in everyday living. 'John, that talk was a personal best.' 'Jean, that meal must be a personal best.' The role of the encourager is a mighty one.

When a group of athletes were asked what they would do if they were offered a drug that would guarantee them a gold medal in the Olympics, a drug which would not be detected, but which would kill them within a few years, more than 50% said they would take it. When I read the findings of this survey I was reminded of a Canadian yachtsman in the 1988 Olympics. During one of the races at Pusan, Mr Lemieux spotted a Singaporean yachtsman in real difficulties. The Canadian stopped, took the victim on board and finished 21st. I am glad that when the Olympic Committee learned of the incident they decided to give Lemieux a special award. He had gloriously fulfilled the Olympic ideal that there are more important things in life than winning 'gold'.

The BMA recently stated that because all meat is contaminated, how it is handled and cooked is all important. Likewise, because we human beings are anything but perfect, how we handle people is also vitally important.

I can think of people who would be happier if instead of giving others a bit of their mind, they were to give them a bit of their heart.

Fair and Stormy Weather

It is reckoned that people spend at least six weeks of their life, talking about the weather!

As I travelled by train through the snow-covered Cairngorms, a representative of the Scottish Tourist Board distributed to the passengers a Scottish Holiday brochure. From the pictures one might well have concluded that all Highland cottages are freshly painted, that there are shaggy Highland cattle in every field, Skye terriers in most homes, and that Scotland is bathed continuously in wonderful sunshine. The impression given was that the weather is the one thing that does not change in Scotland, blue skies with not a dark cloud to be seen. How with all this sunshine the golf courses are so green or the trout streams so full, was not explained.

Not all who visit Scotland leave with this mental image of a land bathed in golden sunshine! An Arab tourist in Scotland had experienced heavy rain every day. On the final day it was still pouring as he took a bus trip to Loch Lomond. Seated next to him on the bus was a friendly Glasgow lady. By the time they reached Balloch at the foot of the Loch, she was struggling to keep the conversation going. Outside it was still raining '*cats and dogs*'. After what was to her an embarrassing silence, she said to the Arab, 'I believe in your country they used to worship the sun.' He smiled and said, 'So might you if you ever saw it.'

In his book *The Change in the Weather* William Stevens points out that the phrase *raining cats and dogs* is a corruption of a saying about how when the rain is heavy, cats want to stay inside and ducks want to get out. At some stage 'ducks' seems to have been so pronounced that it sounded like dogs.

Samuel Coleridge once wrote, 'Summer has set in with its usual severity'. Bob Hope described the British climate as eight months of winter and four months of bad weather. A hundred years ago an equally grim picture was painted of British weather in a poem in *Punch*.

> *January — black and beastly;*
> *February — wind north-easterly;*
> *March — neuralgic, nipping, nasty;*
> *April — pluviose and blasty;*
> *May — wet, prematurely torrid;*
> *June — dull, glacial, Arctic, horrid;*
> *July — delugy and dismal;*
> *August — drowned in floods abysmal;*
> *September — biting, blustrous, boggy;*
> *October — frosty, frowsy, foggy;*
> *November — sort of short, sham summer;*
> *December — cold as June, but glummer.*

That depressing picture of our climate is as misleading as the sundrenched picture painted by the Tourist Board. Personally I am glad we don't have the climatic extremes of other countries. During a three-month summer exchange with a minister in South Florida I recall, shortly after we arrived in West Palm Beach, saying to a resident, 'What a beautiful sunny day.' He looked at me strangely, as if to say, 'What do you expect in the sunshine State?' A few weeks later, as the sun once again shone into our bedroom early one morning, I turned to my wife and said, 'Not another sunny day.' On our return to Scotland it was actually a delight to wear a sweater again, and see clouds rising slowly up the mountainside in wispy layers after a day of rain. What a comforting thing rain can be, refreshing the air and causing the roots to spread in the earth.

Though for many elderly city-dwellers snow is simply a cold slushy nuisance, a slippery hazard, I love the occasional heavy snowfall. It transforms the hills into a shimmering wonderland

and woodlands into places of magic. The evergreens with their great white branches weighted down almost parallel with their trunks, resemble giant birds with their wings folded against the cold. How valuable snow also is, nourishing and protecting the fields, insulating houses and barns against the severe bite of winter. The smiles on children's faces as they set out with their sledges for a snowclad slope, or as they build a snowman in the garden, are a joy to behold. Snow also temporarily erases the worst mistakes of men, restoring lost innocence to a scarred world.

A Glasgow minister had the habit of including in every Sunday morning service a prayer of thanksgiving for the weather. One bitterly cold February Sunday, when the strong wind was driving the sleet almost horizontal, the few members who were present were sure he could not possibly give thanks that morning for the weather. But they were wrong. In his opening prayer he said, 'We thank you, God, that the weather is not always as bad as this.'

On a similarly unpleasant day weather-wise, I met a man from Embo in the Square at Dornoch. 'Mr Simpson,' he said, 'that is a cold East wind, no matter what direction it comes from.'

Numerous are the meteorological excuses for people not worshipping. The weather is either too hot or too cold, or it is too sunny to be cooped up indoors, even for an hour. As an old minister said, 'It takes an extraordinary arrangement of meteorological circumstances to make it possible for some people to come to church.' He pronounced every syllable with deep feeling.

Spring is when the bulbs you did not get round to planting last autumn fail to appear.

A man confessed his irritation with weather reports. 'All I want to know is how warm or wet, calm or windy, it is going to be here tomorrow. But the weatherman keeps telling me about high pressure in the North Sea, or storms off Iceland. Who cares about that?' But we have to care, for distant weather systems ultimately determine our weather. High pressure off the Azores can mean warm weather for us. The strong cold winds off Greenland could well dump inches of snow on our gardens in a few days time. The future of many of the warmest parts of the earth depends on what happens to the coldest parts. The weather, like everything else in God's world, hangs together. But predicting it accurately, even with the sophisticated equipment now available, is another matter. One weather forecaster said that what he saves for a rainy day is an alibi. Having got it wrong three consecutive nights, he said the fourth night, 'Tonight I predict darkness.'

Sir Anthony Eden's father could at times be very undignified. On one occasion, the barometer had forecast good weather for his garden party. But just before it was due to start, dark storm clouds gathered. Shaking his fist in the air, William Eden tore from the wall the barometer which still indicated 'Fair', and threw it out of the window with the cry, 'There, God, see it for yourself.'

Before the days of mad-cow and foot-and-mouth disease, a friend said to a farmer who was always moaning, 'Well, John, you won't have anything to complain about this year. You had fine weather for the lambing and the sowing and then lovely warm days and light rain to germinate the seed. You got a good spell of weather to gather in the hay and the right mixture of rain and sun to ripen the barley, and then another glorious week to harvest it.' 'Aye, that is true,' said the farmer, 'but a year like that fair takes it out of the land.'

A fortnight in Bali, or the Riviera, could be misery if our attitude was not right, or if we were not on good terms with those accompanying us. On the other hand a courting couple are quite happy in the rain. They huddle under the one umbrella, alone and happy in their tiny space. They also love the sun, swimming in the ocean, sunbathing on the sand, running along the beach. Attitude is all important. When you next look out at a gloomy day, remember that it is the day that is gloomy, not you. If you also want to be gloomy that is all right, but it is not mandatory.

Someone once said that there is no such thing as bad weather — just inappropriate clothing. That is an overstatement, but there is some truth in it.

Robert Louis Stevenson, who suffered most of his life from poor health, was once asked the secret of his cheerfulness. 'I have a maxim. Make your own inside weather.'

Ho-Ho-Holy Humour

The old lady was deaf. This meant that the question she asked her minister was asked in a voice sufficiently loud for all in the hall to hear: 'Was entering the ministry your own idea, or were you just poorly advised?'

A minister who was due to conduct a funeral in the afternoon suffered a heart attack in the morning. Even when the ambulance men were carrying him out of the house, he was still protesting that he could not possibly go to the hospital as he had a funeral to take. An hour later as his wife left the hospital, the junior doctor's face was a picture of bewilderment. He had overheard her say to her husband, 'Now don't worry, dear, as soon as I get home, I will phone the undertaker.'

A minister tells of a service where the congregation joined in the prayer of confession as printed in the Order of Service. 'Eternal God, in whom we live and move and have our being, whose face is hidden from us by our *sons..*.' A typographical error of course, the classic prayer reading 'hidden from us by our sins..' When he later shared the new version of the old prayer with his sons, he asked them whether this might explain why saintliness had eluded him.

Students entering the lunch room at a theological seminary were greeted with a sign that read, 'Take only one apple. God is watching you!' At the other end of the table was a large tray of chocolate chip cookies, next to which was a hastily scribbled sign: 'Take as many as you want. God is back there watching the apples.'

In the worship services at the 2001 General Assembly of the Church of Scotland, the Moderator, Dr John Miller, focussed on the Beatitudes. To each of the Commissioners he and his wife Mary gave a small card, the size of a railway ticket, with the Beatitudes printed on it. One evening when some of the Glasgow Commissioners were returning home by train from the Assembly, one of them by mistake handed the ticket inspector the little Beatitude card, instead of his ticket. The inspector looked at it, then said, 'This will maybe get you into heaven, but it will not get you to Glasgow by ScotRail.'

George Burns, the American humorist, recalls his first success as an entertainer: 'When I was seven, I was singing with three other Jewish kids from the neighbourhood. We called ourselves the PeeWee Quartet. A local department store held a talent contest representing all the local churches. When the Presbyterian Church had no one to enter, the minister asked the four of us to represent them. There we were, four Jewish boys, sponsored by a Presbyterian church and our opening song was "When Irish Eyes Are Smiling". We followed with "Mother Machree" and won first prize. The church got a purple velvet communion cloth and each of us got an Ingersoll watch. I was so excited I ran all the way home to tell my mother. She was hanging out the washing. I hollered out, "Mama, I don't want to be a Jew any more." She calmly said, "Do you mind my asking why?" "Well," I said, "I have been a Jew for seven years and never got anything. I was a Presbyterian for fifteen minutes today and I have already got a watch." My mother answered, "First help me hang up the washing and then you can be a Presbyterian." '

The Rev Douglas Nicol tells of a visit by members of the Church's Reappraisal Committee to the island of Gigha. They were due to meet with the church office-bearers to discuss the future of their church. Unknown to the visiting committee, the ferryman was a staunch member of the island church. 'Are you the hatchet men from the church offices?' he inquired. Learning that they were from the church offices, he informed them that if they were of a mind to close the Gigha church, he would not take them back to the mainland! 'In the light of what I have just said, do you want a single or a return ticket?'

Though the phrase 'We're a' Jock Thomson's bairns' is commonly used in Scotland, few know its origin. In the early 1800s John Thomson was the minister of Duddingston Kirk near Edinburgh. As well as being a fine parish minister, he was also an outstanding artist. One of his landscape paintings was recently sold for £60,000. Over the studio door at the foot of the manse garden John Thomson had painted the word 'Edinburgh', so that on a Monday, the day he devoted to painting, his wife could honestly say to callers, 'I am sorry. My husband is in Edinburgh.' Duddingston manse became a well-known meeting place for the literary and art world of Edinburgh. Sir Walter Scott was a regular visitor. For 35 years John Thomson faithfully ministered in Duddingston. He loved his people – all of them, the gifted and the not so gifted, young and old, rich and poor. And they loved him. He would often refer to his congregation as 'My bairns'. They in turn proudly said, 'We're a' Jock Thomson's bairns.'

A sermon helps people in different ways. Some rise from it greatly strengthened, others wake from it greatly refreshed. 'I know well who he is,' said one man about a person under discussion. 'We sleep in the same pew.' They were nodding acquaintances!

A country minister was dismayed to find that several of the farmers in his congregation had a habit of going to sleep in the warm atmosphere of the church. So he worked out a plan whereby every two or three minutes in his sermon, he said in a loud voice – 'God grant...'. On hearing the word 'grant' all the farmers woke up.

Mungo McInnes had a large moustache and beard. All his life he had been a forester. But more than that, all his life he had been a great exaggerator. What stories he made up about his early days. He used to tell the boys in the Ayrshire village of Ballantrae the most fantastic stories, about how as a young man he had been attacked by pirates, how he had been shipwrecked, how he had found hidden treasure and had killed a bear with his own hands. The village youngsters were sure there was no one like Mungo McInnes. One day a teacher in the local Sunday School began her lesson on creation by asking the five-year-olds. 'Who made the world?' One boy replied, 'Mungo McInnes.' The following day the teacher met Mungo and told him what had happened. On hearing the child's answer, Mungo scratched his ear and with a glint in his eye, said, 'Well I suppose I did have a hand in it.' His answer was not as silly as it might at first sound. For better of worse we all have a hand in making the world the kind of world it is. We live in the eighth day of creation.

Dr Stephen Leacock, the American humorist, told how shortly after receiving an honorary doctor of literature from an American university, he boarded a ship for Europe. He proudly signed himself on board as Dr Leacock. That evening there was a knock on his cabin door. When he opened it the steward told him that one of the girls in the Follies dancing troupe seemed to have sprained her hip. Would the doctor be good enough to come and examine her. Said Leacock, 'I was down there like a flash, but not soon enough. Two doctors of divinity had got there before me.'

A Mr Heneghan tells of a traditional Roman Catholic Archbishop in America who was not at all happy at some of the innovations being introduced into worship services by some of his priests, such as dancing Masses. One Sunday he sat beside a parish priest while the choir crooned. Artificial mist poured into the sanctuary. Through the mist there suddenly came dancing the scantily dressed figure of a girl. Gaping at this modern-day Salome, the archbishop turned to the priest and growled, 'Listen, if she asks for a head on a dish, it's going to be yours.'

A minister who parked in a no-parking zone attached the following message to his windscreen. 'I have circled this block ten times. I have an appointment to keep. Forgive me my trespasses.' When he returned he found a note attached to a parking ticket. 'I have circled this block for ten years. If I don't give you a ticket, I lose my job. Lead me not into temptation.'

A young girl confessed to her priest she was guilty of the sin of pride. 'When I look in the mirror I think I am beautiful.' 'That is not a sin,' said the priest. 'That is a mistake.'

Once in a church with a rather uninspiring minister, I listened to a handful of people sing 'Onward Christian Soldiers' with the line, 'Onward then ye people, join our happy throng'. I found it very depressing for not only was there no throng, they were clearly not happy, and they sounded as though they did not really care whether anyone joined them or not. How different was the experience of a British newspaper reporter. The day before she was due to interview Bishop Tutu, she decided to worship in his cathedral. When she told him at the start of the interview how deeply moved she had been by the worship, the African rhythms, the wonderful singing, the colour and drama, Bishop Tutu responded with a twinkle in his eye, 'Isn't worship fun?' Church services ought never to be a big yawn.

Adjacent to a city church there was a popular restaurant. Its kitchen equipment was evidently needing attention, for one day the local doctor noticed a mechanic's truck parked outside the church. The truck carried the sign 'Refrigerated Services'. Being a keen churchman the doctor hoped no would think the sign referred to the kind of services which took place there on a Sunday. Did he perhaps recall what Robert Burns wrote about a church service he attended in Lamington?

As cauld a wind as ever blew;
A caulder kirk and in't but few;
As cauld a minister as ever spak;
It will be a long time ere I'll be back.

It saddens me when I hear of people still being turned off the church because of refrigerated or joyless services.

A visitor once asked the Rev Paul Corcoran how many services he had on a Sunday. I warm to his reply. 'There are two services, both at eleven o'clock. One is too formal, has too many ancient hymns and lasts too long. The other is too informal, has too many modern hymns and lasts too long. There are also two sermons. The one I preach which is brilliant, witty and brief, and the one I hear people say is dull, lifeless and far too long. There are also two congregations at 11 o'clock; there is the one the ushers count, and the one I count. My congregation is always the larger!'

When a minister asked a group of teenagers if any of them planned to give up something for Lent, one responded immediately, 'I intend to give up my New Year resolutions.'

A young Canadian mission worker who was always looking for guidance from the Lord, explained that he had come to South America because when he was considering his vocation, a friend had given him a Brazil nut chocolate bar. 'What would you have done if it had been a Mars Bar?' asked his sceptical friend.

A religious fanatic is a person who does what he thinks God would do if God knew all the facts of the case!

The following intimation appeared in an American church newsletter: 'Six new choir robes are needed due to the addition of new choir members, and the deterioration of some of the old ones.'

A cartoon depicted a car salesman saying to a minister, 'It is a special model for church committees. It comes equipped with one accelerator, four steering wheels and ten sets of brakes.' I have served on such committees, committees that lack not only focus and organisation (four steering wheels), but an unwillingness to try new things (ten sets of brakes).

After serving on many committees, I have reached certain conclusions.

Always arrive a few minutes late. To arrive on time marks you out as a new member.

Don't say anything until the meeting is half over. This will convince the others that you are an intellectual who always thinks before he speaks.

When you do make a comment, don't be specific, for that can irritate others.

When in doubt suggest that a sub-committee be appointed.

Be the first to move for an adjournment. This will make you popular.

An American minister tells how one night at a Session meeting, he sought to clear his holiday dates with the office-bearers. He was speechless when one of them suddenly said, 'I think three weeks vacation is a lot to ask from someone who works only one hour a week.' There was a moment of embarrassing silence before another office-bearer said, 'I move that we give the pastor three hours off!' The motion was carried with one abstention.

It was the first night of a weekend church conference. The chairs were hard. When the evening session finished one man slowly straightened himself up. As he turned round he noticed an elderly couple picking up cushions they had brought to sit on. Pointing to the cushions, he said, 'That was foresight.' 'No,' replied the man, 'Hindsight.'

Being a former Moderator of the Presbyterian Church of Scotland, I enjoyed the story of the proposed Papal visit to Indians in a remote part of Canada. A great crowd of Indians had gathered at the airport. But unfortunately just before the Pope was due to arrive, the fog came down and the plane could not land. On hearing what had happened a Presbyterian minister said to some Indian friends. 'If it had been the Moderator of our church, the fog would have dispersed and you and your fellow-Indians would not have been disappointed.' You are right,' said the Indian. 'My people would not have been disappointed because none of them would have been there to meet him.'

Some time ago a letter was received at the church offices addressed to 'The Second Person in the Trinity, 121 George Street, Edinburgh'. The letter contained an invitation for the Moderator to attend a special function. Apparently what had happened was that a civil servant had been told to send invitations to the heads of the various churches in Scotland. Turning to a colleague, whom he knew was an elder in the Kirk, he enquired who was the head of the Church of Scotland? The elder, more knowledgeable than many, replied, 'The Second Person in the Trinity'. The letter duly arrived on the Moderator's desk. Had it been addressed to 'The First Person in the Trinity', I suspect the church's mailing office would have sent it to the Principal Clerk to the Assembly (*the nearest thing we have to a chief executive*).

Lady Astor told the story of the black preacher who recounted in his vivid way the Creation story. 'Once there was nobody in the world, wasn't white folks or black folks, wasn't nobody and God was lonely. So He got some mud and stood it up against a fence to dry. He then breathed on the mud and made it into a man, and that was the beginning of the world.' Just then a boy's voice was heard to say, 'Mr Preacher, if that was the beginning of the world, who made the fence?' The preacher replied, 'Child, it is questions like that what's just ruining religion.' I could not disagree more. If Christianity is to be a vital force in our lives, we must never stop asking questions.

Someone defined a 'rare book' as one most people have heard of, but few have actually read. The Bible unfortunately has become a rare book. Many today are unfamiliar with its great themes and stories. A friend, Alison Macgregor, tells of going to the Edinburgh Playhouse to see *Joseph and the Amazing Technicolor Dreamcoat*. In the cloakroom prior to the show, a youngish woman asked her if she had seen the musical before. 'It is a great story,' she added. When Alison told her that though she had not seen the show, she had read the story, the woman asked in amazement, 'Is it in a book?'

Joe Leckie was a unique character in the Kirk. Not only was he the tallest minister in the church of Scotland, 6′ 9″ in height, his heart was equally big. As a schoolboy he once captained the Scottish schools rugby team. The team picture, which appeared in the *Tatler*, had the caption, 'Joe Leckie and the fourteen dwarfs'. Joe's first church was in Irvine, in Ayrshire. One night as he was returning home he noticed a small man, rather the worse for drink, staggering home carrying a bag of coal on his back. 'Look,' said Joe, 'let me help you.' Picking up the bag of coal, as though it was nothing more than a bag of sugar, he carried it with great ease to the man's home and deposited it by his back door. The following day Joe discovered the coal had been stolen!

A church matched these songs with Biblical characters:

Raindrops Keep Falling on My Head ...Noah

I Have Got the Right to Sing the Blues ...Job

Stayin' Alive ...Methuselah

The Lady is a Tramp ...Jezebel

When You Wish upon a Star ...The Three Wise Men

A minister tells of an old lady who said to him, 'I always feel the better when you leave.' She could have worded it better.

For me proof that a prayer need not be long is the brief but moving one — 'Lord make me the kind of person my dog thinks I am.'

When the minister asked the wee boy what his cat's name was, he was told it was Ben Hur. When the minister expressed the view that it seemed an unusual name for a cat, the wee lad said, 'Well, we used to just call him Ben, but then he had kittens.'

From a church bulletin comes the intimation, 'Our morning worship will begin at 10.30am and continue until next summer'. Another bulletin listed the opening hymn as 'Immoral, invisible, God only wise'. What made it worse was that the congregation sang it as printed! In yet another church bulletin a line from the Battle Hymn of the Republic appeared as, 'As he died to make men holy, let us diet to make men free.'

In Jerusalem there is a bar just down the street from the King David Hotel. It has a sign which reads, 'Just a stone's throw from the King David.' The name of the bar is 'Goliath'!

Church members were asked to provide whimsical catchy slogans for the outside church noticeboard. Among the better ones were –

After two thousand years, still under the same management.

Come and enjoy live music every Sunday.

Where God is not a swear word.

Visitors welcome. Members expected.

So forgiven, we feel guilty.

Within these walls good things happen to bad people.

We agree to differ; we resolve to love; we unite to serve.

In the American *Presbyterian Outlook*, I noticed an advert for an associate Pastor. It began, 'Imperfect church with imperfect staff seeks imperfect candidate in order that grace may abound.' I liked that. We speak a great deal of the evangelical mission of the church. Perhaps we should speak more of the 'unangelic' mission of the church, for it is a mission conducted by people who are not angels to others who are not angels.

A lady was collecting the Christian Aid envelopes she had distributed earlier in the week. Calling at one house she was met with the response, 'Sorry, my dog ate the envelope.' When the collector told her not to worry, that she had spare envelopes, back came the quick reply, 'It would be no good. The dog would probably eat them too.'

For the church harvest festival, one mother had prepared a basket of fruit, cheese and rolls for her 4-year-old son to give to the minister. When at the beginning of the service the minister took it from him, the wee lad started to scream. His teacher and mother both rushed forward, puzzled as to why he was so upset. Eventually he composed himself sufficiently to whimper, 'That man took my packed lunch.'

On a Church noticeboard there was a checklist for locking the church. 'Put out the lights. Check heaters are switched off. Check doors are locked. Take collection to the night safe...' It was entitled, '**How to close the church**'. A similar list could easily be prepared for church members entitled, '**How to close the church permanently**'.

* Leave everything to the minister and the Kirk's faithful pillars. In most congregations the pillars are outnumbered by the caterpillars, those who occasionally creep in and out!

* Never volunteer for anything. When asked to help say No.

* Protect the status quo. Be like the man who said he was tempted to join the Greek Orthodox Church, because there, change in the fast track takes 400 years!

* Regularly criticise the minister. Always speak of the church's failures and least attractive members, never of her glories or those members who are the salt of the earth.

*   Lay down your gold, frankincense and myrrh at other shrines. Give the church your cheese-pairings and candle-ends.

If all the lukewarm members would fire up,
All the gloomy members would cheer up,
All estranged members would make up,
All the gossip folk would shut up,
All the true believers would stand up,
All those on the roll would show up,
To honour Him who was lifted up;
You would have the world's finest church

–Anon

When a black American minister was asked the secret of his power as a preacher, he replied, 'I reads myself full. I thinks myself clear. I prays myself hot, and then I lets go.'

Shortly before I retired as interim minister at Brechin Cathedral, I was told that a dear old lady in the congregation had said to a friend, 'I had an enjoyable visit yesterday from our intimate minister.'

A few people in their own lifetime capture the hearts and imaginations of their generation. Pope John the 23rd was one of these. On the opening night of the Second Vatican Council which he convened in the 1960s, he stood at the window of his private study in the Vatican, smiling at the thousands of cheering people below in St Peter's Square. Finally he said to them, 'Go home and make love grow from here to everywhere.' One commentator said that it was not too much to say of Pope John what one Gospel writer said of John the Baptist, 'There was a man sent from God whose name was John.'

A wealthy and very pious American, well-known for his often ruthless business dealings, said to Mark Twain, 'Before I die I intend to make a pilgrimage to the Holy Land. There I will climb Mt Sinai and at the top I will read out loud the Ten Commandments.' 'I have a better idea,' replied the writer. 'Why not stay at home and keep the commandments?'

A 6-year-old who had been eating an apple in the back of the car, asked his Dad why an apple core turns brown. His father explained that when the skin is taken off, the inside comes into contact with the air. 'This causes it to oxidise, thus changing its molecular structure.' There was a long silence, before Matthew said softly, 'Daddy, are you talking to me?' I wonder if some worshippers feel the same about preachers who use abstract ecclesiastical language. A young minister tells of how, after just one month of preaching in his first charge, his senior elder took him aside and said, 'Charles, we think we are going to like you a lot, but your sermons are going right over our heads. Remember that the Lord said, "Feed my sheep", not "my giraffes".'

Churchill was so critical of bureaucrats who scorned simple words, substituting 'lower income groups' for poor, and 'accommodation units' for homes, that one day in the House of Commons, on hearing an MP use the latter phrase, he startled his fellow MPs by exploding into song, 'Accommodation unit, sweet accommodation unit, there is no place like accommodation unit'. I am sure he would have been equally critical of the theology professor who began his sermon by reminding a Highland congregation that they were surrounded by 'an apodeiksis of theopratic omnipotence'! I find it significant that Jesus did not say in his famous parable, '...when the prodigal developed a high degree of self-identity, he said to himself'. Instead he simply said, 'And when he came to himself...' I would endorse a suggestion made by C.S.Lewis that before being ordained, church ministers should have to pass an examination in translating the scholarly language of theology into the language of the ordinary person in the pew. Church members ought not to have to take their dictionaries as well as their Bibles to church.

Jingle Bells

James Pierpont died more than a hundred years ago. Most people remember him for only one thing, for a song he wrote about the joys of getting on a big sledge pulled by a horse, and laughing and singing with friends as they speed over the snow. Though this song 'Jingle Bells' is often sung at Christmas, and is now associated in the minds of children with Santa, it originally had no connection with Father Christmas. James Pierpont trained initially as a teacher, but when he found it difficult to control his class, he left teaching and became an organist and choirmaster. He served for some time in this capacity in the church where his brother John was minister. But when he and his brother spoke out against slavery, they were forced to resign. Both felt very deeply for the slaves. All their lives James and John Pierpont thought they were terrible failures. A contemporary said of James when he died, 'He had a relatively undistinguished life.' But I suspect God did not regard as failures these brothers who longed to be loving human beings, who were concerned to make life easier for those finding it very hard, who got involved in the big issues of their day, and who brightened the lives of millions by giving them a song to sing.

When a former Bishop of Chester expressed the view that there should be a religious message on Christmas stamps, *Punch* magazine suggested, 'Lord *deliver* us.'

A teacher in County Derry tells how during a rehearsal for the nativity play, two shepherds came into the stable, knelt down, but said nothing. Suggesting that they should think of something nice to say about the baby Jesus, the teacher made them go out and come in again. As they knelt the second time, one said, 'The baby is lovely, and do you know, Joseph, I think he has your eyes.'

For another nativity play a group of children were being assigned parts. Each had to play an animal in the manger scene. One little lad asked if they could be any animal they wanted to be. The minister thought that since all animals were created by God, it was a reasonable request. 'Goody,' said the little lad, 'I want to be a Tyrannosaurus Rex.'

The film *How the Grinch Stole Christmas* is about an old hermit who lives in the mountains. He was so jealous of everyone in the village having a good time that he decided to sabotage their Christmas, to adopt the role of a reverse Santa Claus and steal all their presents. But because of one little girl who goes on loving him, despite his unloveliness, his heart melts, and he ends up giving all the presents back. But not before the surprised residents of Whoville discover that just spending time with each other, without benefit of the presents, is really more in keeping with the true spirit of Christmas.

An American, Alan Abramsky, tells how under a cultural exchange programme, his family one December hosted a rabbi from Russia. One night when they had finished eating in a Chinese restaurant, the waiter presented each of them with a small brass Christmas tree ornament as a seasonal gift. When someone at the table pointed out that the ornaments were made in India, they all laughed except the rabbi. Tears trickled down his face. When they inquired if he was upset by being given a gift from a Christian festival, he replied, '*Nyet*. I was shedding tears of joy to be in a country in which a Buddhist gives a Jew a Christmas gift made by a Hindu.'

A little boy was puzzled why Mary looked so sad in a picture of the nativity. 'Was she secretly hoping for a girl?' he asked.

A father and his 10-year-old son were looking at a famous painting of the Nativity in an Art Gallery. 'Dad, why is the baby Jesus lying just on a pile of straw?' The father, who was not too familiar with the Christmas story, replied, 'Well son, his parents probably could not afford anything better.' 'Then Dad, how come they could afford to have their picture painted by such a famous artist?'

When he retired from being in charge of Religious Broadcasting in Scotland, Dr Ronald Falconer told of one of his greatest regrets. During a live Christmas Eve broadcast service from Dalmarnock, in the East End of Glasgow, a drunk man had suddenly entered the church. When Dr Falconer noticed two of the elders getting up from their seats and quickly moving towards the inebriated visitor, he was convinced that they were about to evict the man. So he told the camera crew not to film the incident. He was afraid there might be a scuffle, or a loud protest. But instead of evicting the man, the two elders sat down beside him in one of the pews. One of them put his arm gently round him, and the other shared his hymn-sheet with him. Dr Falconer's regret was that he had not captured on camera that wonderful moment when the church lived out its manifesto, 'All Welcome'. Years later Dr Falconer had no recollection of anything the minister had said that night, but he never forgot what he had seen.

In reply to the teacher's question, 'Why was Jesus born in Bethlehem?' one little girl replied, 'Because his mother was there.'

There is food for thought in a poem by Joan Ellison

>*God didn't wear rosy glasses*
>*That first Christmas morn*
>*God knew it was a*
>*chip on the shoulder,*
>*beam in the eye,*
>*dog eat dog,*
>*no room at the inn*
>*kind of world*
>*when Jesus was born.*
>*Our dilemma may be NO TIME*
>*instead of NO ROOM.*

True generosity depends not upon the size of the gift, but upon the love of the giver.

Legend has it that on the night of the Nativity, whoever ventures out bearing a succulent bone for a lost dog, a wisp of hay for a shivering horse, a warm cloak for a stranded wayfarer, a dish of crumbs for huddled birds who thought their song was dead, and 'goodies' for needy children, will receive gifts of 'such astonishment as will rival the hues of the peacock and the harmonies of heaven'.

Reasons why Santa is obviously not a man.

Men can't pack a bag.

They would rather be dead than caught wearing red velvet.

They don't answer their mail.

They are not interested in stockings unless someone is wearing them.

I doubt if Colin McCaffery deserves a prize for his attempt at Seasonal humour. He tells how Good King Wenceslas phones his local Pizza Hut to place an order. 'Will you have your usual?' says the girl. 'Yes,' says Good King Wenceslas, 'Deep pan, crisp and even.'

An American twice stood unsuccessfully for the Senate. Shortly after his second defeat, he was the guest speaker at a dinner. The chairman, in introducing him, spoke of the high regard in which he was held. When the applause subsided he began by saying, 'I would gladly exchange some of that respect for a few more votes.' I suspect Jesus would also gladly exchange some of the

Christmas carolling for a few more votes, for a few more people who would care more and forgive more. 'You call me Lord, but do not the things that I say.'

On almost every page of the diary of an octogenarian was the heart-rending entry, 'No one called today'. It is a grim feeling being lonely at any time, but as Henry Mahler reminds us in a poem entitled *Exclusion*, loneliness can be intensified at Christmas:

> *Christmas this year finds some*
> *folk left in the cold,*
> *not physically perhaps, but in*
> *need of friendship,*
> *excluded by people who are rich*
> *in family and friends,*
> *or by the social forces of*
> *discrimination or class*
> *stratification,*
> *or the very pace and*
> *complexity of our civilisation.*

The Church secretary was embarrassed when a typographical error in the Sunday Order of Service was pointed out. One of the carols was listed as 'Angels we have heard, get high'.

The boss received considerable ribbing from his staff when after Christmas he arrived at the office wearing a very strong and unusual smelling aftershave. When the staff learned that it had been a present from his wife, one of them said, 'She obviously wants to keep all other women at bay.'

For the Western world, the gift giving of the Magi became a dominant theme. Tradition added considerably to the Biblical account. The number of Magi was fixed at three, complete with names, Melchior, Caspar and Balthasar. As the carol 'We three Kings of Orient are...' reminds us, the developing tradition described them as being kings. (There is no mention in Matthew's account of the Wise Men being either kings or three in number. The notion that there were three probably stemmed from the fact that they presented Jesus with three gifts.) In the mediaeval West the Magi acquired nationalities and characteristics to represent the known world – one European, one African and one Mongolian. The Magi became a powerful reminder of the significance of Jesus, not just for the Jews, but for the whole world.

I rather like the 4-year-old's version of the well-known Christmas song, 'We wish you a Merry Christmas and a Happy New You.'

In Britain, a child's introduction to the theatre is often via the Christmas pantomime. In essence it consists of a well-known fairy-tale, updated by topical and local references. The quick-change acts and extraordinary transformations are heightened by audience participation. The Principal Boy is always played by a girl and the Dame by a middle-aged man. Often included in the cast are a few celebrities who, despite an obvious lack of acting ability, have been invited to make the transition to the theatre, people like the boxers Frank Bruno and Barry McGuigan, and the former BBC weatherman Ian Macaskill. Far from youngsters being put off, they seem thoroughly to enjoy their first theatre outing. On the other hand, perhaps it is not all that surprising the pantomime has not caught on in other countries!

I Was There

A painful schoolboy memory is of the method often used in the playground to select sides. The selection process being dependent on sporting ability, not being chosen early on must really have got to the less athletic, for it said something about what others thought of them. The most painful and humiliating experience of all was to be the one left to the end, especially when the sides were even without you. I can still recall one callous captain saying of a delightful but non-athletic classmate, 'I have got all the players I need. You can have him in your team.' To which the other captain responded, 'No it is all right. You can have him.' How that must have hurt.

For four years at Glasgow University I studied maths and physics. Along with a close friend I hoped to do research with the Atomic Energy Establishment. At that time they had two major centres for research – Harwell, which concentrated on the peaceful uses of Atomic energy, and Aldermaston, where major research was being done on Hydrogen bombs. In 1955 the only openings were at Aldermaston. Spending my life designing and creating ghastly weapons of destruction being an unacceptable prospect, I did not pursue my application. My friend Ronnie, who accepted, was soon posted to the Christmas Islands where H-bomb tests were being carried out. On returning to London he wrote me one of the saddest letters I have ever received. In it he told how a major effort had been made to clear out the animals from the islands, but they could not remove the birds. 'I can now claim to have seen 4 H-bombs and lived to tell the tale. It is quite exciting for a time, but the casualties we find later are upsetting, birds blinded, scorched and hopelessly bashed about, still walking and hopping about, screaming in agony. I do not have the heart to put them out of their misery... It would be nice to be able to say that we have left that island behind forever... It is such an evil place...' Birds screaming in agony is bad enough. God forbid that it should ever be men, women and children.

When in 1958 I first visited the United States, I sailed on the *Queen Mary*. Then it was considerably cheaper to sail than fly. When the liner docked in New York Harbour at 8am, there started the lengthy process of disembarkation. The first class passengers were given priority. Then the cabin class passengers, and then those of us who were travelling tourist. In the medical department a doctor closely examined our X-ray plates which, at that time, it was mandatory to carry. In the agricultural department we were given the option of either eating any fruit we had, or handing it over to the American authorities. This process helped identify the Scottish passengers. They were standing eating the fruit!

It was after eleven before I was finally clear of immigration and customs. Having made arrangements for my luggage to be delivered to the college where I was to be studying for a year, I caught a bus to Times Square. My intention was to explore a bit of Manhattan. But there, surrounded by flashing neon lights and milling crowds, I suddenly felt desperately lonely. I knew no one in New York or the States. So I quickly decided to proceed without delay to the college where at least my name would be known. Stopping a little man who was passing, I asked him how to get to Broadway at 120th Street. Instead of answering my question, he said, 'Are you from Scotland?' I had not previously realised my accent was so marked. When I told him I was from Scotland and just off the *Queen Mary*, he said, 'Are you in a hurry?' Now during the voyage, I had been reading all about the gangster life in Chicago and New York, and here was a total stranger asking if I was in a hurry! Taking into account the fact that he had a kindly face, and was smaller than I was, I indicated that I was not really pressed for time. 'Well, let me buy you your first American lunch.' Hailing a yellow cab, he took me to a delightful restaurant.

When he learned during lunch that I had been thinking of doing some sightseeing, he said, 'If you are not in a hurry, let me introduce you to the Big Apple.' After phoning his office, he hailed another taxi. At Madison Square Gardens he introduced me to the manager as his Scottish friend. Then we visited the Broadway theatreland, the Empire State building and the United Nations – all by taxi. About 5 o'clock he suggested it might be helpful if he introduced me to the New York Underground. Paying my ticket, he rode with me to the college. At the door he wished me a happy stay in the States. Before he left, I inquired why he had taken so much time off his work to welcome a total stranger. At first he was reluctant to answer, but finally said, 'I have never been in Scotland, nor as far as I know have I any Scottish ancestors. [With a name like Joseph Dunay, he was probably right.] But during the last war I was in Europe, and there two of my best friends were Scotsmen. Unfortunately both were killed. I am only repaying you a little of what your fellow Scotsmen meant to me.' You can imagine how deeply moved I was. Fourteen years later I was benefiting from the lives of two unknown fellow countrymen, soldiers who had enhanced the reputation of their native land by the way they lived and died.

In 1991 I was invited to do a television interview with Harry Secombe in Skibo Castle, the stately summer home which Andrew Carnegie, the American multimillionaire, had built. We were to discuss the church's attitude to humour, and explore my reason for writing books of humour, to raise funds for Cystic Fibrosis research. The producer felt it would add to the programme if, half-way through the interview, my 5-year-old granddaughter Sally , who suffers from C.F., came and joined me. At the end of the interview Harry posed for a photograph with Sally on the magnificent castle staircase. Later that week I posted him an enlargement of the photo, for him to sign for Sally. Returning it duly autographed, he asked if he could possibly have a copy for his own scrap album. To accompany the photograph, Sally wrote a card, 'With love from Sally'. Three days later a florist delivered the most beautiful bunch of flowers. The accompanying card read, 'To my little friend Sally. Thanks for the photograph. Love Harry.' That was typical of the man. He really did make goodness and Christianity attractive.

Many years later the television programme *Everyman* told the inspiring story of Harry Secombe's magnificent fight to overcome a major stroke. Viewers were left in no doubt that his strong faith, great courage and wonderful sense of humour were powerful factors in his recovery. That programme recalled how prior to my own interview with Harry, we had an opportunity, while the lights and cameras were being positioned, to share anecdotes and experiences. When Harry laughed it was as though his whole body was getting a massage. When at one stage I commented on his signet ring, he told me that engraved on it was his own coat of arms, and personal motto, 'Go On'. With a twinkle in his eye, he said, 'You can read it as "Goon" if you like.' During our conversation he recalled how when he was knighted by the Queen, he had to return his passport to be amended. He was sure they would issue him with a new one, but instead he received back the original with the words, 'Now SIR', inserted before his name. On a visit to Thailand a few months later, the immigration officer, having examined and stamped his passport and having inquired about the nature of his visit, smiled and said, 'Have a good holiday, Nowsir.'

When the popular children's television programme *Blue Peter* decided in 1997 that its Christmas Appeal would be for Cystic Fibrosis Research, Sally, who by this time was eleven, was approached to see if she would be willing to be interviewed for one of the programmes, to be screened in the weeks leading up to Christmas. The film crew, having recorded an interview in the hospital in Inverness between Sally and her consultant Dr Macdonald, informed my daughter that they would be arriving the following morning at 7am, to film Sally getting her treatment and getting ready for school. When the producer that day met the family's fourteen-year-old dog, he asked my daughter if she would allow him to film Sally taking the dog for a walk on Dornoch's glorious sandy beach. The idea was that as she walked along the beach, she would tell the viewers about her treatment, and how C.F. had affected her medically and socially. Even though their old dog was blind, deaf and unable to walk very far, my daughter agreed. What lovely pictures the film crew managed to get. When the programme was screened nationally, my wife and I phoned Sally to tell her how well she had done and how proud we were of her. When my wife then added, 'Our only worry is how your dog is going to cope with all this national publicity,' Sally replied, 'Yes, it is worrying. She has already had a phone call from one of the Queen's corgis.' How we laughed. What a joy to see her lively sense of humour developing.

For a year my wife and I lived above the Georgian House in Charlotte Square in Edinburgh. The residence of the Moderator of the General Assembly of the Church of Scotland, was for many years on the top two floors. On the afternoon of the opening day of the Assembly we were leaving for the Garden Party at Holyrood Palace. The big limousine with flag flying was waiting at the door. I was resplendent in Moderatorial attire, and Helen was wearing a new outfit. At the door of the busy Georgian House were two little boys. Having noticed the limousine, and the way we were dressed, one of them said, 'Are you two going to get married?'

On one occasion a guide in the Georgian House noticed an elderly woman furtively manoeuvring her shopping bag near a table on which were exhibited four rare Georgian wine glasses. As the woman hurried out, the guide dashed to the table, to find there a fifth glass, an exact replica of the original four!

During our Moderatorial visit to London, my wife and I visited the Royal Caledonian School. As we were being shown round I noticed, beside the bed of an 11-year-old boy, Kevin Anderson, a large cartoon drawing of John Major playing cricket. When I happened to mention to Kevin that I was going to visit the Prime Minister the following day, he said, 'Do you think he would like to have my drawing?' I had no alternative but to say, 'I am sure he would.' The following afternoon I set out for 10 Downing Street with Kevin's drawing in a large envelope. Fortunately I had met John Major on two previous occasions in Scotland, so we were not total strangers. In the Cabinet Room I said, 'Prime Minister, I am slightly embarrassed about this, but I have promised a young boy that I would give you a cartoon drawing of yourself.' Having looked at the drawing he said, 'It really is very good. I have certainly seen many worse cartoons of myself.' At the close of our official meeting we went upstairs to join our wives for afternoon tea. The Prime Minister took the drawing with him and showed it to his wife who was of the same mind, that it was very good. I later received a letter from the headmaster, enclosing a copy of a letter the Prime Minister had sent Kevin.

Dear Kevin,

The Moderator of the Church of Scotland came to see me today and he gave me the picture that you drew of me as a cricketer. It is a very clever piece of work which I enjoyed. Thank you for letting me have it. By the way I noticed that the cricket bat is decorated with the colours of Scotland. Perhaps one day you will be good enough to play for Scotland. I hope so.

Yours sincerely, John Major.

The headmaster's letter said, 'I am writing to thank you for making a young lad with behavioural difficulties very happy. The letter which he received from the Prime Minister has made him something of a celebrity and given him a sense of achievement. His behaviour has greatly improved. Instead of getting into mischief, Kevin now spends a great deal of his time painting and drawing.' I never cease to marvel at the transforming and motivating power of a word of praise.

One of the earliest weddings at which I officiated was the marriage of two Inspectors of taxes. Countless tax stories were told at the reception. By far the best concerned a farmer who had been dodging paying Income Tax. One day out of the blue he received a demand note from the Tax authorities for £1,000, a princely sum in the early 1960s. Very upset, he asked his neighbouring farmer what he should do. 'If I was you, John, I would pay it, for you know and I know that you owe the Income Tax much more than £1,000.' When the farmer finally decided he had no alternative, he went to the tax office in Stirling with the demand note and a hundred ten-pound notes. Placing them firmly on the desk, he said to the girl, 'That is the last I want to hear about that.' As he made to leave, the girl said, 'Just a minute and I will give you a receipt.' With a puzzled look on his face, he said, 'You don't mean to say you are putting that through your books.'

During a visit to Richmond in Virginia, I was taken one Sunday to a beautiful old house near Charlottesville called Redlands, a home owned by a Bobby Carter and his wife. As we drove up the long driveway, I had the strange feeling that I had seen this house before, even though I had never previously been in that part of America. The feeling grew more intense as we drove past the former slave cabins and the old oak tree at the front door. It really was a strange feeling of déjà vu. After dinner in the old kitchen with the dumb waiter, which again all seemed so familiar, we adjourned to the porch. There Bobby Carter told me how two years before, the BBC had asked for permission to use his home to film the story of the early years of Nancy Astor. Mirador, her real childhood home, had been modernised and was near a noisy motorway. What made Redlands so familiar was that just prior to leaving for the States, I had watched the BBC documentary about Lady Astor. How relieved I was.

On a later visit to Redlands, Bobby Carter took us to see Thomas Jefferson's home Monticello, near Charlottesville. The house, designed by Jefferson, is a most impressive building, but what made the deepest impression was the inscription on Jefferson's tombstone in the grounds of Monticello. The words were penned by Jefferson before he died. 'Here lies Thomas Jefferson, author of the Declaration of Independence, of the Statute of Virginia for religious freedom, and father of the University of Virginia.' Had he forgotten that he had also been President of the United States? The service he had rendered in the cause of truth and freedom was obviously more important to Jefferson than presidential status.

I am a recent convert to the world of cyberspace. My conversion stemmed from the realisation that unless I overcame my ignorance about computers, I was going to get left high and dry on the beach. In a well-stocked bookshop I asked for a copy of *Computers for Dummies.* When the assistant inquired for what program I wanted the instruction manual, I replied, as graciously as I could, 'I don't know! You see, I am a dummy.' Is it fair to expect Dummies to know that there are different programs, much less how one program differs from another? Perhaps a new approach is needed – a book for those who like to become dummies!

In 1981 I was invited to conduct worship for the Royal family at Crathie Church. The invitation was accompanied by a letter inviting me to spend the weekend at Balmoral Castle. Having passed through security at the Castle gate, I was told to drive to the North door where a policeman would show me where to go. But when I arrived at the North door there was no policeman to be seen. Not wanting to begin the weekend by going to the wrong door, I consulted the little map I had been sent. While I was doing this, a lady in an anorak and headscarf, who was walking on the lawn, called over and told me that if I went in the North door, I would find the equerry who would direct me. I waved and shouted thank you. An hour later I was taken to the drawing room to meet the Queen. When she entered I bowed and said, as instructed, 'Delighted to meet you, your Majesty.'

A big smile came over her face, 'Oh, but we have already met. I was the friendly policeman who gave you directions outside!' That night we had our evening meal in a log cabin in the nearby hills. There were no staff present, just the Queen and Duke, members of their family, including Charles and Diana, who had just returned from their honeymoon, and Margaret Thatcher and her husband. The Duke was in charge of the barbecue. Diana and the Queen acted as waitresses serving the tables and clearing away the dishes. It was a truly unique occasion. The following morning I was seated in the breakfast room when Diana entered. Coming over to where I was, she said, 'Would you mind if I join you?' I doubt if any man in Britain would have turned down such an offer. Diana being three days older than my daughter Morag, who had been married a few weeks before her, we had a most relaxed conversation. When we parted the thought uppermost in my mind was that I was glad Morag would not be subjected to the kind of pressures Diana was already experiencing.

During a later visit to Balmoral, I was seated at Sunday lunch between Princess Alexandra and the Duchess of Kent. The Princess being the royal patron of the Cystic Fibrosis Trust, we naturally spoke about the Trust and my granddaughter. When I told her Sally was a keen member of the Brownie Guides, and that for her collector's badge, she was gathering the postcards my wife and I were sending her from the various towns and countries we were visiting in my capacity as Moderator of the General Assembly of the Church of Scotland, she said to my surprise, but delight, 'Would she like me to send her a postcard?'

When I assured her Sally would be thrilled, she got a postcard and wrote, 'To Sally with love. Princess Alexandra.' The Duchess of Kent, who had overheard our conversation, asked if I thought Sally would like her to send her a card as well. Again I assured her Sally would be delighted. So she got a postcard and wrote a similar message. Seated opposite us at the table was Norma

Major, the Prime Minister's wife. When she inquired about the reason for the postcards, I explained about Sally. 'Would she like me also to send her one for her collection?' she asked. Having obtained and written the postcard, she went to the top of the table and got her husband John to sign it as well. You should have seen the look on Sally's face when the postcards arrived. Sending these postcards involved a minimal amount of effort for the Prime Minister and his wife, the Princess and the Duchess, but what tremendous joy they brought Sally. Being a typical 8-year-old, she not surprisingly asked her mother if she could take them to school to show the teacher!

That evening the Queen shared with me a lovely story about her state visit to Malta in 1992 to commemorate the 50th anniversary of the granting of the George Medal to Malta. (I had forgotten that in the late 1940s, before she became Queen, she had spent several years in Malta while Prince Philip was serving in the Navy.) Shortly after the Royal Yacht berthed in Valetta, she was driven in a motor cavalcade down the main thoroughfare. From the car, she noticed at the side of the road a lady with a placard which read, 'I am Jessie's daughter'. Her initial thought was that the woman must be mentally unstable, but a minute later, in an excited tone, she said to Philip, 'That was Jessie's daughter.'

For four years Jessie had been their landlady in Malta. What a wonderful landlady she had been. The Queen had become very fond of her, and her daughter. Occasionally during school holidays Jessie's small daughter would accompany her mother. The Queen hoped that on the return drive through Valetta, Jessie's daughter might still be there. She was not disappointed. Again she raised her placard, 'I'm Jessie's daughter'. Although unable to stop the cavalcade, she asked the driver to contact the police and get them to invite her to come to the *Britannia* early that evening. The half-hour they spent together, recalling fond memories of Jessie, was for the Queen one of the highlights of her Malta visit.

The Later Years

Of late I have been getting the impression that nature is conspiring against me for the financial benefit of chiropractors, chemists, chiropodists and dentists. In fact the price of dentistry is such that the phrase '*putting your money where your mouth is*' has taken on a new meaning for me. I have reached that stage in life when everything is beginning to click – elbows, knees, neck, back. I can sympathise with the man who said it was now such an effort to stoop down and tie his shoelaces, that he asked himself if there was anything else he could do when he was down there.

'Can you remember when we used to chase the girls?' said one old man to his friend. 'Yes, but I cannot remember what for.'

The wit and charm of Adlai Stevenson, the former US ambassador to the United Nations, made him a constant target for autograph hunters. Once as he left the UN building in New York and was as usual surrounded by young admirers, a small elderly woman in the crowd held out her autograph book and said, 'Please, Mr Ambassador, could a very, very old lady have your autograph.' 'Delighted,' Stevenson replied with a smile. 'But where is she?'

When a bright, attractive 89-year-old was asked what her secret was, she replied, 'When I was sixty I looked over my shoulder one day and saw old age catching up with me. So I just stood aside and let it pass.' You begin to age when regrets take the place of dreams.

A newly retired man was being kept busy round the house by his wife who had gone on a spring-cleaning binge. He had tidied up the garden, washed the windows, cleaned the gutters, and he was exhausted. Feeling that he was entitled to a rest, he eased himself into his armchair. His wife, hearing the creak of the springs called out, 'Are you sitting down?' He replied, 'Yes, dear. But it is all right – I am not leaning back.'

The Psalmist describes us as being 'fearfully and wonderfully made'. Commenting on that verse, a middle-aged woman with a lively sense of humour, said, 'I accept the description "fearfully made" for I am reminded of that fact every morning when I look in the mirror. What I see there is truly a scary sight. But "wonderfully made" presents more problems.' Then she added, 'My least favourite hymn is *Look ye saints, the sight is glorious.* Not in my mirror!'

At the age of 20 we worry about what others think of us. At 40 we don't care what they think of us. At 60 we discover they often haven't been thinking about us at all.

In middle age we are always looking for bigger and greener fields. Old age is when we have given up looking for bigger fields because we cannot even mow the one we've got.

I have the feeling Francis Bacon was overstating the case when he said in commendation of great age – 'Old wood is best to burn, old wine to drink, old friends to trust and old authors to read.' Old age also has some drawbacks! I can sympathise with the friend who said, 'Trying to stay healthy is just about killing me. Jogging has ruined my knees. Lifting weights has strained my back. Swimming has rewarded me with sinusitis.'

One of the few drawbacks of retirement is that it does take some of the fun out of Saturdays.

Elderly people are like plants. Whereas some go to seed, or to pot, others blossom in the most wonderful ways. I believe beauty competitions should be held only for people over seventy years of age. When we are young we have the face and figure God gave us. We did nothing to earn our good looks. But as we get older, character becomes etched on our face. Beautiful old people are works of art. *'Like a white candle in a holy place, so is the beauty of an aged face.'*

When old folk dress in unconventional ways, or are not over-concerned about what they wear, they are often diagnosed by amateur psychiatrists as becoming senile. But if this is the criterion for senility, we will have to certify many young folk who dress like scarecrows. One day on a bus in Edinburgh a young man with a mohican haircut, with rings in his ears and eyebrows, and wearing torn jeans, sat down opposite an old woman. They were facing each other, their knees almost touching. The young man was chewing away furiously at gum. When the old lady made to leave, she said very politely to the young man. 'Thank you for talking to me, but unfortunately being hard of hearing I did not hear a word you said.'

Two elderly ladies had been friends for many years, sharing all sorts of adventures and activities, but they were now limited to playing cards together once a week. One day one of them looked at the other and said, 'Now don't get mad at me. I know we have been friends for a long time, but I cannot think of your name right now. What is it?' Her friend stared at her and sat in silence for a few minutes before finally answering, 'How soon do you need to know?'

When from time to time I do stupid things, like going into a room to get something, and forgetting when I get there what I have come for, I take comfort from the fact that Isaac Newton, one of the greatest scientific minds of all time, was found one day in his kitchen holding an egg and boiling his watch. I also derive comfort from a story about 'Rabbi Duncan' as he was affectionately known in University and Church circles. He was a professor of Hebrew early last century. One evening his wife appeared dressed, all ready to go out to a social engagement, which he had forgotten. Admonished by his wife he hurried upstairs to change. As he was a long time returning, his wife went to investigate and found him in bed. As he was changing, his mind wandered off and from force of habit he finished up in his pyjamas and bed.

The ancient proverb, 'Whom the gods love die young', does not mean what many think it means, that those whom the gods love are taken from this life in their youth. It means that those whom the gods love retain the gift of essential youth even when well on in years. It is far better to be seventy years young than forty years old.

The great art of living is to die young as late as possible. When someone asked the elderly John Quincy Adams how he was keeping, he replied, 'Thank you. John Quincy Adams is very well, but the house in which he lives is falling to pieces. Time and seasons have nearly destroyed it. The roof is well worn, the walls are shattered. It trembles with every gale. I think John Quincy Adams will soon have to move out. But he himself is very well.'

An American minister, the Rev David Steele, died recently after a lengthy battle with cancer. Writing from the hospice, he said, 'I am living now in a strange new world. I call it Gehenna. All my life I have lived by the tongue – preaching, telling stories, doing skits. Now I find myself in a community where most are hard of hearing. That for me is Gehenna. My wife says it is good for me to listen and of course she is right. But boy, it is a tough transition.'

When George Burns was in his eighties, he said, 'There is nothing that I cannot do now which I could not do at eighteen. That shows you how pathetic I was when I was eighteen.' On another occasion he reminded his audience that with a good positive attitude and a little bit of luck there is no reason why we can't live to be a hundred. 'And once we have done that, we have really got it made, because very few people die over a hundrd.'

Lord Brougham, one of the founders of the *Edinburgh Review*, and at one time Lord Chancellor of Great Britain, carried into old age some of the exuberant qualities of a schoolboy and some of the enduring traits of a screwball. Twice he announced his own death, just for the fun of reading the obituaries. Unfortunately we have no record of whether he liked what he read. His joke finally rebounded, for when he did die, some newspapers, having been fooled twice, did not print anything.

The person who says he is too old to change, probably always was.

A wealthy man who retired at fifty played golf every morning, weather permitting. Then he had his lunch. In the early afternoon he often went swimming or to the gym. Then before his main meal he dozed a little. Then he either played bridge or read or watched television. Although often approached, no one could get him to engage in voluntary work of any kind. His great slogan was 'One must keep fit.' One wanted to ask, 'Fit for what?' He seemed not to realise that the value of life consists not in its duration, but its donation.

When Konrad Adenauer, the first Chancellor of the Federal Republic of Germany, was in his late eighties and still Chancellor, he caught a heavy cold. His doctor, who was unable to do much to relieve his symptoms, had to put up with Adenauer's impatience. 'I am not a magician. I cannot make you young again.' 'I don't want you to,' retorted the Chancellor, 'All I want is to go on getting older.'

A maiden lady who was a member of Grace Episcopal Church in Madison, Wisconsin, left very specific instructions for her funeral. 'There will be no male pallbearers. They would not take me out when I was alive; I don't want them to take me out when I'm dead.'

A few suggestions for enriching retirement:

If there is a hobby you have long thought you might like to try — try it.

Cultivate your sense of humour. On life's journey from nappy rash to denture adhesive, humour is a great pain reliever.

Enjoy long walks, remembering all the times you were too busy to have them.

Spoil your spouse first — then you can both spoil your grandchildren.

Don't let television become your favourite pastime.

If you know it all, pretend you don't.

Don't make the subject of who has died or who is dying a regular part of your conversation. Make it rather part of your private prayers.

If you get a tax refund don't spend it all on groceries.

Don't regret growing older. Remember that a lot of the sugar is to be found at the bottom of the cup! Remember also that growing older is a privilege denied to many. The alternative is not good for the complexion.

Avoid becoming a 'groan' up, living your later years in the 'objective' mood!

The Feather in His Cap

In the States I am often asked, 'Where do you come from?' When I reveal that I come from Scotland, the questioner will often say, 'How wonderful.' Scotland seems to be one of those countries whose reputation gladdens the heart. Sometimes these same people go on to ask, 'What part of Scotland do you come from?' When I reply, 'The Highlands,' their eyes light up even more. You are given the clear impression that to be born Scottish and to live and work in the Highlands, is to have won first prize in the lottery of life. Perhaps they are not far wrong.

> If the earth is God's cap
> Surely the Dornoch Firth is
> The feather in His Cap.

If you are looking for beauty of form, colour or sound, or breathtaking panoramic views and quiet golden beaches, or outstanding golf courses, the Dornoch Firth has no equal. In Scottish and world golf, Royal Dornoch Golf Course occupies a distinctive place. The American steel magnate, Andrew Carnegie described this northerly part of Scotland as his 'Heaven on Earth'. Others have called it, 'Scotland's Shangri La'. To view the Kyle of Sutherland from Struie Hill is to feel sure that 'earth has not anything to show more fair'.

The following is a selection of stories about the area, and some lovely Dornoch people who for the most part are unknown outwith Sutherland. I have also included some fascinating stories about the better-known Carnegie and Sutherland families. The golf stories will have to wait for another book.

In the opening chapter of his novel, *Dark the Night, Wild the Sea*, Robert McAfee Brown tells of a visitor to Eriskay in the Western Isles. Meaning to compliment the locals, he said, 'You have a beautiful island. But it's so far away.' On hearing this, a man called Angus inquired in melodious tones, 'Far away from where?' Angus' question recalled how a visitor to Dornoch was once overheard to say, 'Dornoch would be a fine place to live, if it was not so far from the centre of things.' A Dornoch lad viewed things differently.

Returning from a spell of work in London, he told a friend, 'London would be all right if it was not so far out of the way.'

A holidaymaker one Monday went into the newsagent in Dornoch, and asked for a copy of the *Times*. The girl who was new to the job, told him that the *Times* was not in until Thursday afternoon. Whereas she instinctively thought he was referring to the local paper, the *Northern Times*, the Londoner instinctively assumed everybody thought of the *Times* as the London *Times*. Where is the centre of things? That is not a question for astrophysicists or geographers. The centre of things is where love is. We feel at home where we are surrounded by people we love and people who love us.

The town of Dornoch grew up round the Cathedral. Its central location still serves as a reminder that what happens in the shops, offices, schools and police station on Monday is as important as what happens in church on Sunday. When Dornoch Cathedral was built in the 13th century, erecting great churches and Cathedrals to the glory of God was what was deemed most worth doing. In the 19th century, building railways was the thing deemed most worth doing. In the early 20th century it was roads and motorways. In the latter part of the century it was building great shopping malls. Those who designed and built Dornoch Cathedral sought to reproduce in the stone pillars and soaring arches something of the majesty of God's great forests, the impressive natural aisles created by avenues of trees. I marvel at the skill of those who in these early days caught a bit of heaven and wove it into stone. The Cathedral gives you the impression that everyone involved in it had a whale of a time. It is as though the masons and the woodcarvers gave a great shout, 'Let's go!' as they soared off into the realm of great art, beauty and colour. I hope they derived considerable satisfaction from knowing that they were giving to the world something that would outlast their frail bodies.

The surroundings and traditions to which we are exposed when young affect our outlook more than we often imagine. Ruskin rightly observed that every bright boy in Edinburgh is either consciously or unconsciously influenced by the sight of the castle. I am sure that is also true of Dornoch youngsters, for the mediaeval red sandstone Cathedral, floodlit at night, and the old Bishop's Palace (now the Castle Hotel) are so central to the town. Andrew Carnegie, who as we have noted, chose to spend a large part of his later years in the Dornoch area, tells how affected he was by the abbey in his home town of Dunfermline. Recalling the day when he set out with his father and mother from Dunfermline in the hope of his father finding employment in America, he wrote, 'I remember that I stood with tearful eyes looking out of the window until Dunfermline Abbey vanished from view. During my first fourteen years of absence, few days passed in which I did not see in my mind's eye, the talismanic letters on the Abbey tower, **King Robert the Bruce**.'

Andrew Carnegie was well into his fifties before he married. He was 62 when his only child Margaret was born. That momentous day he said to his wife Louise, 'This little girl must have a little Scottish home.' Though he had made his fortune in America, he had never lost his love for his native land. Shortly afterwards he came to the North of Scotland, and purchased the Skibo estate, a few miles from Dornoch. There he set about building the baronial castle of his dreams. Once the magnificent building was finished and furnished, he invited the world's nobility to come and enjoy his hospitality. The visitors book at Skibo Castle was like a 'Who's Who'. Among the signatories were the Polish pianist Paderewski, the composer Edward Elgar, the Rockefellers, King Edward VII, J.H.Taylor, the five times Open golf champion...

I remember one day asking Margaret who of all the visitors had most impressed her. She said there were three. She recalled how Rudyard Kipling took her on his knee and told her the Jungle Book stories. 'His eyes,' she said, 'were as fascinating as his stories.' Then there was Booker T. Washington. Margaret's father had been so impressed with this black man who had begun life as a slave, that he helped finance the Tuskegee Institute, one of the first colleges for black students in America. Mr Washington became its president. Margaret described him as one of the loveliest men she had ever met. She proudly showed me what he had written in her autograph book, *'My dear young friend, I have learned that success is to be measured not so much by the position that one has reached in life, as by the obstacles which one has overcome while trying to succeed.'*

There was also Helen Keller, who was rendered deaf, dumb and blind at the early age of 19 months, yet lived one of the most useful lives of her day. She stayed overnight at Skibo with her companion Anne Sullivan. Margaret recalled the serenity of her face, and how she stood at the dining room door before dinner and felt the faces of those who were to share the meal, thus building up her own mental picture. In the morning her companion, by moving her fingers deftly over Helen's hands, informed her that a piper was playing outside. Having transcribed what Anne was saying to her by means of touch, Helen went to the drawing room window and put her hands on the glass. Suddenly a great smile came over her face, 'I can hear the bagpipes.' Through the wonder of touch she could detect the vibrations. Once when Helen was addressing people who could see and hear, she said, *'Use your eyes as if you would be one day stricken blind. Apply the same method to your senses. Listen to the music of voices, the songs of birds, the mighty strains of an orchestra as if you would be stricken deaf tomorrow. Touch each object as though tomorrow your sense of touch would fail. Smell the perfume of the flowers, taste with relish each morsel, as if tomorrow you would never smell or taste again. Make the most of every sense, glory in all the facets of pleasure and beauty which the world reveals.'*

To the man in the street the name Carnegie was synonymous, not only with vast wealth, but with free libraries. He gifted 3,000 libraries to cities and towns as widely scattered as Dornoch, Dallas in Texas and Dunedin in New Zealand. The conditions for such a gift involved the city providing a suitable site for the building, and guaranteeing a certain sum each year for its future support. An amusing article in the Dunedin newspaper in 1902 makes interesting reading. 'Mr Carnegie has offered Dunedin £10,000 for a Free Public Library. What a gold mine Mr Carnegie must have fallen upon. We have a relative of his living in Dunedin and one or two of his schoolmates in the country around. One of the schoolmates was home in Scotland some time ago, and paid a visit to the great multimillionaire. John being in humble circumstances was somewhat afraid to visit Skibo Castle. But at length he summoned up courage, and called at the castle in tweeds, cardless and dusty. "Is the maister in?" queried John. "Yes my man," replied the bedecked porter; and with this he invited him to sit down outside the door. A little later a footman came and told John to go round to the office at the back of the castle. The look of contempt on the footman's face, John has not forgotten. Well round to the office John went, and there, among several gentlemen, stood Mr Carnegie. "Weel Andy, and hoo are ye?" says John. Everyone stood amazed. "Do ye mind Peggie's Brae and Tom Boon?" referring to another school-mate in the Primary school at Dunfermline. With this Mr Carnegie grasped John's hand and shook it warmly. "Man, ye're Jock," says Mr Carnegie, "but I heard you were dead years ago." "True, true," said John, "but I cam' back dead frae New Zealand tae see ye." John was then introduced to all the gentlemen around, and invited to stay at the Castle. He says he had grand times at the Castle, a servant to look after him, a piper to play him into bed and out of bed, flunkeys to touch their hats to him, dishes that he was afraid to name, table utensils that he knew not how to use, chairs in which he was afraid to sit, and carpets to tread upon; but one thing of which he was not afraid and at which he was delighted to chuckle, was that "peacock o' a footman wha pointed me to the office wi' his nose". John is loud in Mr Carnegie's praises, and says he is withoot doot the finest man he has ever met.'

Having gifted so many libraries, Carnegie not surprisingly wanted a good library for himself in the castle. Lord Acton was given the job of selecting the books and Hew Morrison, the librarian of the Carnegie Library in Edinburgh, the job of making the purchases. Carnegie wanted it to look like a working man's library, not a rich man's hobby-horse. He was angry when he received a bill from Morrison for rebinding the books in magnificent gold, brown and green bindings. He did not hide his displeasure in the letter he wrote.

I asked you to get the best editions of a list of books Lord Acton would furnish you. I never said one word to you about changing the bindings of these gems. Now I learn that you have spent more money on bindings than the precious gems cost. This to my mind is not only a waste of money, but an insult to the great Teachers from whom I draw my intellectual and emotional life, my spiritual existence. I really am hurt by this affair.

I doubt if there was ever a private library so beautiful or as under-used as the Skibo one. The books stood on the magnificent hand-carved oak bookshelves in resplendent condition. When seventy years later I was privileged to use the library, I had to cut many of the pages in the books. Many of them had obviously never been read.

A few years after being called to be minister in Dornoch, I was told that the Cathedral pipe organ was in need of a complete rebuild. Having just finished major repairs to the roof of the Cathedral I did not look forward to trying to raise in a small community the kind of money involved in such a rebuild. The poor state of the organ was revealed when the BBC decided to do a *Songs of Praise* broadcast from the Cathedral in the late 1970s. The producer, himself an accomplished organist, broke the news that the organ was in a deplorable state. In fact the BBC agreed to go ahead with the recording only provided an organ builder was on hand to carry out any repairs that might be required. For the Church magazine I penned a brief note about the state of the organ, entitled 'Good News, Bad News' – the good news being that the BBC were going ahead with the broadcast, the bad news being that very soon we would have to rebuild the organ. Shortly after the magazine was produced, I got a phone call from Margaret, Andrew Carnegie's daughter. Each year, like her father and mother before her, she spent eight months in the States and four months in the summer in Skibo Castle, during which time she was a regular worshipper in the Cathedral. On the phone she told me there was something she would like to discuss with me. As we chatted in front of the castle log fire, she said, 'I believe you are having problems with the Cathedral organ.' The organ had been one of the 7,000 pipe organs her father had gifted at the turn of the century. I assured her that what she had heard was correct. 'Well,' she said, 'I am an old lady now and there is not much I can do for the Cathedral, but I appreciate what you are trying to do. The least I can do is give you a new organ. How much do you need?' I took one deep breath and told her how many thousands of pounds we needed. To my even greater astonishment she said, 'Would you pass me my handbag?' Taking out her chequebook she handed it to me and said, 'Jim, you know my eyesight is poor. Write yourself a cheque for what you need.' That day I wrote the biggest cheque I had ever written. Then she said, 'If you give me it, I will sign it.' Having done this, she looked me straight in the face and said, 'I am giving you this on one condition, that you make me a promise that you will get me out of the poor house if ever I finish up in it.' I unhesitatingly made that promise.

I have an old letter written by a Canadian minister to a friend in Dornoch. 'I was greatly interested to get your letter and news of Dossie Grant. I met her once when I was a small boy. I remember that as a girl she was refused her token for communion because she showed an unseemly levity in going to ask for it with a flower in her hat. She may also be aware that as my mother was born in 1843, the year of the Disruption in the Scottish Church, neither the Established nor the Free Kirk minister would baptise her. As governor of the Dornoch prison, my grandfather attended the Cathedral, but his wife, being thrawn, worshipped in the Free Kirk. Neither of the ministers would baptise the child of whom one parent went to the wrong church. My mother was therefore baptised in the prison cell by a minister who was expiating the offence of being "drunk and disorderly".' They obviously had their marriage, ministerial and baptismal problems in 'the good old days'.

While in Dornoch I used to think of January and February as the 'Tired Months'. The icy roads and cold dark days took their toll. One

January morning a man from London phoned a businessman in Dornoch about nine o'clock. He began by inquiring what kind of day it was in Dornoch. The response was immediate. 'It is still night here.' Every year tolerance was in shorter supply during the tired months. The doctor's surgery was more crowded, absenteeism from work was greater. I would love to know whose crazy idea it was to add an extra day to February every leap year. Surely it was sheer masochism to take the perfectly good extra day which God gives us every fourth year and use it to prolong February. Twenty-eight days are more than sufficient for a month I am tempted to call Februweary! Could not the necessary adjustment to the calendar every fourth year have been made by adding an extra day to May, when the days are longer and the countryside so fresh and lovely?

The Spring lambing and the in-gathering of the harvest in the Autumn are the busiest times for Dornoch farmers. Nothing must be allowed to interfere with these all important seasons. This was highlighted by the remark of a Dornoch farm labourer Jack Ross. Within months of war being declared in September 1939, most of the able-bodied young men had volunteered to join up. They all assembled on the Mound station platform waiting for the South train. It was a moving time for all concerned, emotional farewells being said to girlfriends, wives and parents. A comment of Jack's brought a little light relief. 'Could that b–– Hitler not have waited until the harvest was in?'

A town girl who married a Sutherland farmer found the early months of their marriage very trying. Farm life was totally new to her. She was not accustomed to getting up at the crack of dawn, let alone having to prepare meals for the farm workers. When her husband one morning came into the kitchen and announced that the cart load of turnips outside the kitchen window were for the cattle, she started to sob. 'John, I cannot possibly peel all these.' I was also a 'townie' when I first arrived in Dornoch. Words like tup (ram), gimmer (year-old ewe), grilse (young salmon) and boorach (muddle) were new to me. Determined to learn more about country life, I asked a local farmer Gordon Rutherford if I could come lambing with him one morning. He readily agreed. The arrangement was that I would meet him at the farm the following morning at 6 am. About 5 o'clock the phone went. It was Gordon's wife Betty. She told Helen, who answered the phone, that it was blowing a blizzard outside, and that I should wrap up well. Lying comfortably in a warm bed, I said to Helen, 'Tell Betty I will come another morning.' By 9 o'clock shame was consuming me. I felt I must go to the farm and apologise for being a fair-weather shepherd. The snow was still falling, the freezing wind still blowing hard. As I reached Proncy farm, I saw Gordon and Betty and their daughter Hazel coming down from the hill, soaking wet, each with a newly born lamb under their jacket. Some words of Isaiah came to mind. 'He shall gather the lambs in his arm and gently lead those that are with young.' The Rutherfords had done just that. I had not.

When you mention the *Coffee Pot* to people who have lived in Dornoch for many years, they do not think of Nescafé. They think of the little train that used to run, or perhaps we should say crawl from Dornoch to the junction at the Mound with the main North-South line. It was not the speediest or smoothest journey in the world. Countless gates had to be opened and shut by the guard. Each gate had a different key. The story goes that on one occasion when an American was travelling on the train, the train suddenly screeched to a halt. Looking out of the window he asked the guard what was wrong. 'It is a sheep on the line.' The sheep having been removed, the train travelled on for another few minutes before coming to a halt once more. Lowering the window again, the American inquired whether it was another sheep on the line. 'No,' said the guard, 'the same sheep!'

Not far from Dornoch is the beautiful Dunrobin Castle, the home of the Earls and Dukes of Sutherland, and Carbisdale Castle on the banks of the River Shin, now Scotland's most palatial Youth Hostel. The story of the connection between the two castles is a fascinating one. The 3rd Duke of Sutherland, George Granville

William Leveson-Gower, a big man with a bushy grey beard, was one of the wealthiest peers in the realm. He was also a close friend of the then Prince of Wales, later to become Edward VII. His wife Duchess Anne was lady-in-waiting and Mistress of the Robes to Queen Victoria. The 3rd Duke, who enjoyed driving locomotives and fire engines and sailing his steam yacht *Sans Peur*, had a mistress, May Blair, the wife of a Major Blair. May accompanied the Duke on many of his fishing trips to Florida where he owned a large villa. Upset by this relationship, the Duke's wife took her son, and went and lived in Torquay. Queen Victoria was so upset by the Duke's infidelity, that she never again visited Dunrobin. Shortly after Duchess Anne died, Major Blair died in a shooting accident! This meant the Duke was now free to marry Mrs Blair, which he promptly did. The people of Sutherland were very reluctant to refer to his second wife as the Duchess of Sutherland. They called her Duchess Blair instead. When the Duke died a few years later, the Duchess thought she would inherit all. But unknown to her there had been a reconciliation between father and son. When the Will was opened, she discovered there was a codicil attached leaving a considerable amount to the son. In a fit of rage she tried to burn the codicil, but the lawyer managed to rescue it from the fire. This gave rise to the Sutherland Will trial, as a result of which she was sent to Holloway prison. According to the will she was however given the life use of Dunrobin castle. This meant the 4th Duke was effectively excluded. He and his wife lived in England until they got Duchess Blair to agree to leave Dunrobin. They offered her a very considerable financial settlement if she promised to leave the Castle and never again to set foot in Sutherland. Slightly mad as well as bad, she started building Carbisdale Castle, right on the border of Sutherland with Easter Ross, so that the Sutherland family would be reminded of her every time they travelled south by train. She died before the castle was completed. What a costly act of spite it was.

Before the Dornoch Bridge was constructed, the quickest road to Dornoch was over the Struie Hill. On that road there was a famous observation point on a mountain road. On a clear day the view of the Kyle of Sutherland from the Struie Hill was quite breathtaking. But there were other days when the mist blotted out this glorious view. On such days I used to find it helpful to remember that the blue sky and the hills were still there, even though you could not see them. Likewise in life when the mists drift across our view, it is helpful to recall the lessons learned when the tide of faith was running strong. The Psalmist often did that. 'These things I remember as I pour out my soul. How I went with the throng and led them in procession to the house of God with glad shouts and songs of thanksgiving ... Why are you cast down O my soul and why are you disquieted within me? Hope in God for I shall again praise him, my help and my God.' Memory has helped many see their present depressed situation in perspective. When C.S.Lewis' wife died of cancer, shortly after they were married, he was helped to endure that awful experience by recalling certain high points in his spiritual journey. Recalling yesterday's clear skies can help us endure today's fog.

When I left Dornoch in 1997, I greatly missed not only the Cathedral and its magnificent golf course, I missed also the people of the Royal Burgh, quality people like Helen Kruger, Donnie Macdonald and Mike Burnett. Though Helen Kruger was no stranger to suffering and setback, she was one of the town's cheeriest people, always game for a laugh. Several years ago she gained considerable notoriety. One morning after her early morning cup of tea and toast, she decided to hang out her washing before setting off on her home-help duties. Aware that a piece of toast had lodged itself under her denture, she carefully took it out and placed it beside the washing basket. To her horror a seagull swooped and carried it away. Running into the house she wakened her husband. 'Walter, a seagull has stolen my denture.' When Walter finally came to, he said, 'How on earth did it ever get it out of your mouth?' When the local paper got hold of the story, they printed a cartoon of a seagull with dentures. Underneath was the caption, 'Have you seen this bird?' The *Sunday Post* was the next to tell the story. The following day a London paper contacted her asking if they could send a reporter and photographer to interview her. She graciously refused saying she had already had more than enough publicity. When five minutes later they phoned back offering her a sum of money sufficient to cover the cost of new dentures, she agreed, but still with some reluctance.

For many years Donnie Macdonald was the Sheriff Clerk in Dornoch. But he was better known as the bird man of Sutherland. For more than 60 years he recorded the movements of birds in the area. In his youth he had been a keen badminton player. When no longer able to play, he became a badminton referee. On one occasion he was refereeing a tense match between Dornoch and Brora. Local prestige was at stake. Unknown to him and to the others present that night, one of the ladies in the Dornoch team had been suffering from a gum disease and had to have all her teeth extracted. Her dentures had been fitted just a few days before the match. That night as she went up to the net to smash the shuttlecock, she let out what we would call a Monica Seles grunt. Not only did the shuttlecock fly over the net, so also did her dentures. There was complete silence in the hall.   Finally Donnie broke the embarrassing silence by announcing, 'First set to Brora!'

Our Golden Retriever loved the Dornoch linksland, except when the jets were swooping low over the town, heading for the nearby Tain bombing range. Then Corrie would start to tremble. One day she was trembling to such an extent, that I took her visiting with me. At Creich farm I let her out of the car while I called on the farmer and his wife. I was half-way back to Dornoch when I suddenly remembered I had left Corrie at the farm. Quickly turning the car, I headed back to Creich. Half-way there, I spotted Corrie panting furiously as she ran along the A9. What a welcome she gave me. For the rest of the journey her tail wagged furiously like a haywire metronome. The following Sunday in speaking to the children about leaving things behind, I told them about Corrie. At the end of the service, Mike Burnett, one of my finest members, told me that I should not feel too badly about forgetting our dog, as the previous day, at the end of a shopping trip with his wife to Inverness, fifty miles way, he had driven back to Dornoch *alone*. The impression I got was that, when he finally picked her up two hours later, Alison had understandably not been quite as understanding as Corrie, or as effusive in her welcome.

For sheer natural beauty, and for variety of mountain and coastal scenery, Sutherland is probably unsurpassed – the wide-open spaces and untamed landscape, the stunning jagged peaks, the primeval knuckles of bare rock, the sandy beaches, the brilliance of colour, the yellow broom and gorse in the spring and the purple heather in the autumn. On a clear day every mountain, corrie and glen stands out sharply. One understands what Byron meant when he wrote of 'conversing with Nature's charms' and 'viewing her stores unrolled'.

Helen and I loved the magnificent Dornoch beach, and the sea breezes that often painted colour on our cheeks. There is a spaciousness about the sea, an immensity about its stupendous rhythms, a hint of the everlasting about its vastness. The sea reminds us of the vast and mysterious interdependence of things – the winds, tides and currents all combining to shape our coastlands – the flight-paths of the birds above, and the movements of the fish below the surface. What lessons the sea has to teach; the importance of respect – the sea does not suffer fools gladly; the importance of patience – you cannot hurry the tides, geared as they are to the movements of the moon and the stars. Walking by the sea was a constant reminder that our lives ought to be geared to an ampler rhythm than the tick of the clock. People sometimes smile when they read of the mediaeval monks punishing their own bodies. And yet I often wonder if any monk ever punished his body as much as some of us do today. Many seem prepared to suffer ulcers and coronaries for the sake of getting on, and making a name for themselves.

Waste of Muscle, Waste of Brain

In Sydney, Australia a famous war memorial depicts three women standing shoulder to shoulder holding aloft in their outstretched arms the body of a soldier. The first woman is clearly the soldier's mother, the second his wife, and the third his daughter. The memorial is a powerful reminder that in time of war not only are members of the armed forces killed, but an immense amount of suffering and sorrow is experienced by loved ones. Studdert Kennedy, the outstanding army padre, expressed it well.

> *Waste of muscle. Waste of Brain*
> *Waste of Patience, Waste of Pain*
> *Waste of Manhood, Waste of Health*
> *Waste of Beauty, Waste of Wealth*
> *Waste of Blood, Waste of Tears*
> *Waste of Youth's most precious years.*

Because of a clerical error, a child of two years of age was once summoned to serve on a jury. I cannot help thinking that was a divinely inspired mistake, for in one sense the child is the jury before whom civilisation must be tried. The final test of any society is what it does to children, and allows to happen to children. During a Moderatorial visit to Great Ormond Street hospital in London, the children's hospital that benefits from the royalties from J.M.Barrie's *Peter Pan*, my wife and I met and spoke with a brave little girl from the former Yugoslavia. The previous year Irma had been the focus of the world's attention. *Operation Irma* was the name given to the mission to bring severely injured children from the devastated Yugoslavia to Britain for medical treatment. As a result of a mortar attack that killed her mother Elvira, little Irma suffered severe spinal and head wounds. Irma died shortly after we spoke with her. Seeing grown-ups suffer is bad enough, but children, shocked and scared, longing for their dead mother's embrace, that is different. They don't know what it is all about. In the 4th century BC, the Greek dramatist Euripides depicted war, not in terms of a soldier armed to the teeth, bristling with armour and courage. He portrayed war rather in terms of a woman with a dead baby in her arms. He thus reminded his contemporaries that war is not simply grown-ups slaying one another, but the maiming and destruction of the minds and bodies of countless children.

The September 11th terrorist attacks on America revealed the terrible depths to which human nature can sink. The enormity of these callous, chilling and obviously carefully planned attacks cannot be overestimated. Here was thoughtless disregard for the lives of the innocent. The Twin Towers catastrophe also highlighted, however, the triumph of the human spirit and the heights to which human nature can rise. An unusual amount of bonding took place that day in devastated lower Manhattan. Strangers not only talked to one another. They put their arms round each other. Nominal neighbours suddenly became real neighbours, helping each other cope. Food was shared, wounds were bound up, suggestions offered. The tenderness exhibited was in marked contrast to the previous preoccupation with making a 'fast buck'.

What bravery was shown by the New York fire brigade, rushing towards the burning towers with little or no thought for their own safety. For many of these 'ladder day saints' it was sadly their last act of bravery and courage. Within minutes they were engulfed in the rubble of the collapsing buildings. The alchemy that turns leaden human beings into pure gold was at work. In such hours, when our eyes are blurred with tears, many gain a sense of what is important and what is of secondary importance. The loss of the shiny new car in the car park, or the missed appointment are nothing, so long as family and close friends are safe. The survival of costly business computers is secondary to the survival of those who operate them. The massive overload on the phone system was not caused by people inquiring about the possible effect of the attack on the stock market, but by people calling from the scene of the tragedy to reassure loved ones that they were all right, and by those with loved ones working in the Twin Towers or the Pentagon trying to find out if they were all right. I was reminded of how a man once left his wife a quick note saying how much he loved her. He thought no more about it. Years later he was astonished to discover the note, well-thumbed and dog-eared among her possessions. What a pity that in normal everyday life people are often so reluctant actually to say or write, 'I love you.'

When an American priest, Father Daniel Murphy, lost his younger brother Edward in the terrorist attack on the Twin Towers, he was asked if he was filled with anger. 'Not anger,' he said, 'Sadness yes, at having lost a brother, and a great sense of pain for my mother, for Edward lived with her, but not anger.' He went on to tell how two nights after the attack he took a long walk just to be alone and cry if need be. As he walked he saw a pick-up truck with bright lights and the sound system blaring. The truck was festooned with American flags. At the back there was a big sign which read, 'Kill those damned Arabs and fry them all.' That intensified his sadness, for he and his brother had wonderful Arab friends. The following Sunday he said to his New York congregation, 'Put an American flag on your car or outside your house if you want. Display it with pride, but please not pride in guns, not pride in bombs, or high tech weapons of revenge ... Let our national flag be a symbol of pride that we are a people who have always welcomed the stranger, and not shut out those different from ourselves.'

In a book about World War I, *All Quiet on the Western Front,* the author describes an assault in which he leapt into a shellhole. There to his intense shock, he discovered a British soldier. His instinctive reaction was to bayonet him. But when he saw that the soldier was seriously wounded, he drew back. Instead of killing him, he gave him a drink from his water bottle. The dying man then indicated that he would like the German to open his breast pocket. On doing so an envelope containing pictures of his family fell out. The German held them up one by one and talked to him about his family, until finally the soldier's body went limp in his arms. The change in the way he viewed the British soldier markedly affected how he treated him. At first he was only the wearer of a uniform, an enemy. But later he came to see him as a husband and father, greatly loved by his wife and children.

At the end of the First World War, there were in Europe thousands of graves on which had been carved the words 'Known only to God'. One night, under cover of darkness, four of these graves were opened and the coffins exhumed. One was then selected by an officer who had been blinded in the war. With solemn pageantry that unknown soldier's coffin was received back in Britain. On its way to Westminster Abbey, it was carried past the Cenotaph in Whitehall at the very moment when that Cenotaph memorial was being unveiled. On top of the coffin lay a Field Marshal's baton. For that day the unknown soldier was given the highest rank.

What happened that day was in a sense the beginning of a new age — the age of the common man. The ordinary person was coming more and more into his/her own. Many of the people who continue to steady our country, people to whom we owe a tremendous debt, are also unknown — school teachers who manage to touch off something in a pupil's mind or heart; a parent somewhere who tends the green plant of childhood and gives it strength; a stranger who utters some phrase that takes hold, a nurse who touches a fevered brow ... I sometimes suspect a person's real worth is in inverse proportion to the publicity and notoriety he or she receives.

In the late 1930s Martin Niemöller was one of the few people who had the courage to speak out against the horrors of Nazism. His great regret was that he had not spoken out earlier. When at the end of the war he was released from the prison camp, he wrote, 'In Germany the Nazis came for the Communists, and I did not speak out because I was not a Communist. Then they came for the Jews and I did not speak out because I was not a Jew. Then they came for the trade unionists and I did not speak out because I was not a trade unionist. Then they came for the Catholics and I was a Protestant, so I did not speak up. Then they came for me. By that time there was no one to speak for anyone.'

Abraham Lincoln once said that his two quarrelling sons were a symbol of our troubled world: 'I have three walnuts and each boy wants two.'

Of a well-known boxer it was said, 'He did nothing in his life but fight. How sad that he should have been so articulate in such a dangerous language.'

One night as Willie was doing his homework, he looked up and said, 'Mum, how do wars begin?' 'Well,' she said, 'The First World War began because Germany overran Belgium.' At this point her husband interrupted her. 'That is not how it began at all.' Upset at being contradicted, she said, 'Look, Willie did not ask you. He asked me.' Equally upset by this time her husband said, 'Well for goodness sake tell him the facts and not fairy tales.' To which his wife angrily replied, 'Why must you always interrupt? Nobody asked your opinion.' Finally Willie interjected, 'It is all right. I think I know now how wars begin.'

During the terrible winter of 1942-43, a bomber base which had been hacked out of the English countryside was a sea of mud. People were cold and miserable and many sick with fear. When one officer who was more cheerful than the rest was asked how he could possibly be so cheerful in such awful circumstances, he replied, 'When the facts won't budge, you have to bend your attitudes to them.' Very few people get their first choice in life. What is second best, we can accept with grace and cheerfulness, or with anger and resentment. The apostle Paul chose the first course. 'I have learned in whatsoever state I am, therewith to be content.'

I have never forgotten an American clergyman, Dr Steimle, telling a story about a friendly Jewish tailor he knew in New York. He and his wife had fled the Nazi terror in the 1930s to find a new life in America. One day he said to Dr Steimle, 'I have a problem. My wife, you know, she is a Christian. Her brother, who was a Nazi, hated us when we were in Germany because I was a Jew, and because his sister had married a Jew. He did nothing to help us. But now he is in a prison camp. He writes my wife asking us to help him, to send him something. My wife, she says "No, we send him nothing." But, Dr Steimle, I think we should send him something. What do you think?'

While still in his twenties, Dostoevsky was suspected of being involved in a plot against the Tsar. He was arrested, tried and sent as a convict to Siberia. For four years with chains round his ankles, he toiled in the awful cold, half-starved, filthy and exhausted. All through these years Dostoevsky observed the best and worst in others. His brain stored up impressions, incidents, conversations. Later when he came to write, he drew on knowledge which he had gained at terrible personal cost. His novel *The Brothers Karamazov* is a classic example of what a religious novel ought to be — not so much a novel about religious experience, but rather a novel, the reading of which is itself a religious experience.

During the First World War some soldiers in Europe wanted to have a worship service. Their leader was a man called 'Tubby' Sargent. He was very likely a cheery person, for usually only such people get such nicknames. Well they got a tumbledown ruined cottage, screened the windows with sacking, stuffed up the little holes with turf, so that the light would not show and make a target for the German guns. They then sang some of the soldiers' favourite hymns. Then a man who had never prayed before in public, led them in prayer. Thereafter Tubby took out his little New Testament, and opening it, read the passage about the storm on the Lake. Then he said, 'I don't know if you chaps ever noticed that it says in that passage, *"There were with him other little ships"*. Well, I want to think with you about these other little ships. It would be no joyride for them.' His sermon preached by the light of a few flickering candles was listened to in staggering silence. Outside war raged, but inside was peace and two dozen men thinking of the other little boats who were with them on the sea of life, wives and sweethearts, children and parents, who had been tossed about too.

In *The Unknown Soldier and His Wife* Peter Ustinov has the archbishop pray to the God Mars, 'O mighty Mars, Creator of Widows, fount of tears, lend us your ears in your infinite mercilessness, and hear our prayers. Give us this day our daily victim, and teach us to kill without compassion, so that our civilising mission may go unhindered by cries of mercy or the yells of the despondent. Blind us to charity and deafen us to entreaty, forever and ever. Amen.'

Words are so much more than just sounds in the air, so much more than little black marks on pages. What power they have to make us laugh or cry, love or hate, give up or fight on. In the 1940s Churchill's words brought new hope to a depressed and frightened nation. Anyone could have said, 'Let us be brave.' It took an artist with words to etch on the minds of millions that memorable picture of a defending army giving ground, but never giving up. 'We shall defend our island, whatever the cost may be, we shall fight on the beaches, we shall fight in the fields and in the streets, we shall fight in the hills; we shall never surrender. Let us therefore brace ourselves to our duties and so bear ourselves that if the British Empire and its Commonwealth last for a thousand years, men will say, "This was their finest hour."'

Eivind Berggrav, a former Bishop of Oslo, was one of the outstanding figures of the Second World War. When, in 1940, the Nazis occupied Norway, he immediately helped organise resistance to the Quisling Government. Each week he penned a letter to the members of the Norwegian church. By means of a vast underground movement the letter was distributed and read on the Sunday. These letters, which were strongly critical of the Nazis and all that fascism stood for, greatly upset Vidkun Quisling. His problem was heightened by the fact that he suspected that if he imprisoned Berggrav, there could well be an uprising in Norway and that was the last thing he or the Nazis wanted. So instead he summoned Berggrav to meet with him. When the armed guards brought Berggrav into his room, Quisling signalled to the guards to leave. Then taking his revolver from his holster, he placed it on the table in front of him. 'Now,' he said to Berggrav, 'we can talk on equal terms.' Going into the inside pocket of his jacket, Berggrav took out his pen and placed it in front of him. 'Now,' he said, 'we can talk man to man.' It was that pen Vidkun Quisling feared. To speak, as we sometimes do, of 'mere words' is like speaking of mere dynamite.

Miscellaneous Stories

Early last century, a greatly loved doctor spent all his working life in a depressed mining community. In these days you had to pay to consult the doctor. With his little black bag he went to the miners' cottages to deliver babies, or to wait out the last hours of patients he had treated for years. As he himself lay dying he said to his son, 'In the bottom drawer in my filing cabinet, you will find all my accounts. Take out the unpaid ones and burn them.' The son did as instructed. Shortly after his death the family lawyer inquired about outstanding accounts so that the money could be collected and figure in the estate. But the son had to say, 'There are no outstanding accounts.' They were literally all ashes. In death as in life his father's concern had been to lighten the burdens of those who found life hard.

A father and son were on a golfing holiday. By mistake they entered the clubhouse by the wrong door. Even though they apologised, they were bawled out by a club official. The lad was more upset than his father. He felt his father should have given the club official a piece of his mind. But his father simply smiled and said, 'James, if a man like that can stand himself all his life, surely I can stand him for five minutes.' How often I have recalled that remark when I have had to deal with very difficult people.

When W.H.Smith was at the War Office, his private secretary noticed that on the Thursday before any long weekend, his chief would pack a despatch box with the papers he required and carry it home himself. His secretary one day remarked that Mr Smith would save himself a great deal of trouble, if he was to leave the papers to be put in an office pouch and be sent registered mail to arrive the following day. Mr Smith looked almost ashamed for a moment, but then he said, 'Well, the fact is this. Our postman who brings the letters from Henley has plenty to carry. He is an elderly man. I once watched him coming up the driveway with my heavy pouch in addition to his usual load, and I determined in future to save him as much as I could.' An action like that reveals a certain attitude – the attitude which believes that we should treat others, not as the law allows, but as caring love suggests.

For seven days in the finest hospital in Massachusetts a wealthy Jew called Finkelstein had received treatment for chest pains. Then without warning or explanation he checked himself out and booked into a much inferior Jewish hospital in New York's Lower East Side. The doctor there was intrigued by his decision. What was wrong with Massachusetts General? Was it the doctors, or the nurses? 'No,' said Finkelstein, 'the doctors were geniuses, the nurses angels. No, I could not complain.' 'So it was the food?' said the doctor. 'No, I could not complain about the food. The meals were wonderful.' 'Well, tell me, Mr Finkelstein, why did you leave one of the greatest hospitals in the world to come here?' 'Because here,' said Finkelstein with a smile, 'here I *can* complain.'

Sam Levenson told how his parents were immigrants to America from wartorn Europe. They had fallen under the spell of the dream that the American streets were paved with gold. 'But,' said Sam, 'when my father got to America, he found out three things – the streets were not paved with gold; the streets were not even paved; and he was supposed to do the paving.'

A Kelly Conley tells how on her wedding day she discovered she had a wonderful ally in her mother-in-law. The 3 o'clock start came and went as the guests waited in the church. One of the ushers finally went up to the bride's mother-in-law to explain that the reason for the delay was that they had misplaced the ring. On hearing this she exclaimed, 'That boy would lose his head if it wasn't screwed on.' 'Oh no,' he corrected her, 'it was Kelly who misplaced it.' 'Poor dear,' her mother-in-law sighed, 'she has had so much on her mind.'

A man tells how his sister had decided to wear her mother's wedding dress. Trying it on the first time, it was found to be a perfect fit. When his mother's eyes welled up with tears, he reminded her she was not losing a daughter, but gaining a son. 'Oh, forget about that,' she said with a sob. 'What is upsetting me is that I used to fit into that dress.'

Tuberculosis was *the* killer disease early last century. A Dr Waksman who had left Russia and settled in America made it his life's goal to find a cure. For 27 years he worked in his laboratory, sometimes 7 days a week and 12 hours a day. Finally he isolated the wonder drug streptomycin. Several years later, he was awarded the Nobel Prize for medicine. In Sweden the King presented him with the prestigious award. At the end of the award ceremony, he processed out of the hall with the other prizewinners. Standing at the door was a little girl with her father. She was carrying five beautiful red carnations. Approaching Dr Waksman she said in English she had specially learned, 'One is for each year of my life that you saved.' Apparently the consultant who had been treating the little girl had read about the new American drug. He arranged for it to be flown to Sweden. To the amazement and joy of all concerned, she fully recovered. These five red carnations meant more to Dr Waksman than all the fame and money he received. They made his sacrifice of time and effort well worth it.

A group of people were one day discussing a man who because of an economic depression had fallen on hard times. When one lady remarked, 'The savings of his lifetime have all been swept away,' a wise old man in the group said, 'No, he may have lost his money, but he has retained his pleasure in living. He has made large investments in other lives. These have not depreciated, but are yielding a large return to society today.' Then he added, 'We don't have to worry about him. Let us worry rather about ourselves if the savings of our lifetime are such that they can all be swept away in an economic depression.'

Professor Sandy Raeburn, the professor of Genetics at Nottingham University, was for many years the President of the

Scottish Cystic Fibrosis Research Trust. He told me how on one occasion when he and his wife were to be presented to royalty, his wife insisted that he get his hair not only cut but shampooed. While washing his hair the young hairdresser inquired where he worked. When he told her that he worked at the University, she asked which department. When he informed her it was the Genetics Department, she said, 'That has to do with bunions hasn't it?' As graciously as he could he said, 'Not really.' Quite upset the girl said, 'It has so. My great-grandfather had bunions, my grandfather has bunions and my father also has them. That is genetics, isn't it?' He had to admit she was right. Never before had he heard his work described in this way.

One Saturday Madge Harrah received a chilling phone call telling her that her brother and his family had been killed in a car crash. Madge and her husband decided they would leave the following morning with their young family to be with her elderly parents. Her husband then phoned a lady who taught alongside his wife in the Sunday School, explaining why his wife would not be there the following morning. A few minutes after making this phone call, the other teacher's husband arrived at the door. 'I have come to clean the family's shoes.' Madge never forgot that simple practical offer of help. Later she said, 'Now when I hear of an acquaintance who has lost a loved one, I no longer call with a vague offer of help such as "Let me know if there is anything I can do". Now I try to think of some specific task that suits the other person's need at that time. When that person sometimes asks, "How did you know I needed that done?" my standard reply is, "Because a man once cleaned our family's shoes."'

The Talmudic rabbis tell a lovely story to explain why the Holy Temple in Jerusalem was built where it is. Once there were two brothers who loved one another very much. The younger brother had a wife and four children. The older brother who never married, lived alone. The brothers were farmers. They worked hard to eke out a living on the small farm their father had left them. Each year at harvest they divided the produce. Each took his share and stacked it outside his own house. Once the older brother woke in the middle of the night and was troubled. 'It is unfair for me to take half the harvest. My brother has a wife and children to feed. I should give my brother a larger share of the harvest.' So in the middle of the night he secretly carried a share of his harvest to his brother's house. Meanwhile the younger brother also awoke from sleep troubled. 'All these years I have been equally dividing the harvest with my brother. But this is not fair. I have a wife and children to comfort me. When I am old they will help take care of me. But he will be alone with no one to support him.' So in the middle of the night he carried part of his share of the harvest and deposited it with his brother's share of the harvest. Neither knew what the other was doing so each was amazed that despite his efforts to give part of his own share to the other his own share never seemed to be depleted. This continued for some time until finally one night the brothers met. Each quickly understood. They embraced and wept in love and joy. When God saw this, he decided to have his Holy Temple built on the spot where the brothers met.

John Macdonald, an elderly patient in a frayed dressing gown, shuffled back and forth in Ward 7 of the geriatric hospital. It was the aimless movement of a frail old man who had outlived most of his contemporaries. Suddenly he heard his name being called. He stopped and turned slowly. It was a nursing auxiliary who had called, an auxiliary who was pushing a tea trolley. There followed a mumbled conversation. Disbelief, then joy, then determination registered on old John's face. He had been conscripted to hand out the biscuits. The old man shuffled but one could tell from the spark that had returned to his eyes that he had been momentarily touched by grace. He was once again of use. The auxiliary pointed down the hospital ward and said, 'John, we have to go all the way down to the end. Will you manage?' 'Honey,' he replied in a cracked voice, 'I'd go to the end of the earth with you.' That nursing auxiliary deserved an honours degree in psychology.

During a visit to the States, my wife and I visited the historic Service Creek Presbyterian Church in Western Pennsylvania. The church property borders an attractive little lake. Three large crosses stand at the edge of the lake. At the Easter morning sunrise service the congregation sits on the grassy slope overlooking the lake. The minister conducts the service with the three crosses and the lake behind him. During the service one Easter, a mother duck swam past followed by several little ducklings. When a large bass fish surfaced and swallowed one of them, an audible gasp was heard from the congregation. The gasp was even louder when a minute later another duckling was swallowed. Had I been present that day, my sympathies would have been not only with the mother and her ducklings, but also with the minister who was totally unaware of what was distracting the congregation. All eyes were focussed on the lake waiting to see if a third murder was going to be committed. Few if any were listening to the proclamation of the Resurrection.

A man was being cross-questioned as a witness in a poaching trial. 'Did you see the shot being fired?' asked the judge. 'No sir, I only heard it.' 'That evidence is not satisfactory,' said the judge. 'Stand down.' The witness turned around to leave the witness box. As soon as his back was turned, he shook his head and laughed loudly. The judge, indignant at such contempt of court, called him back and asked how he dared laugh in court. 'Did you see me laugh, your honour?' 'No but I heard you,' said the judge. 'Your honour, that evidence is not satisfactory,' the man retorted. This time everybody except the judge laughed.

An oriental story tells of a man who went to his neighbour to borrow a rope. The neighbour responded, 'I cannot let you borrow it since I am about to use it to tie up a pile of sand.' 'There is no way you can tie up a pile of sand with a rope,' said the man. 'Yes you can,' he replied, 'You can do almost anything with a rope when you do not want to lend it.'

Specialisation has gone so far that today when two professors from different scientific or medical fields meet, almost the only thing they can say to one another, and be understood, is 'Let's have a drink.'

Wanting complete silence to write, the Scottish philosopher Thomas Carlyle built a soundproof room. The only extraneous sound was that of his neighbour's cockerel. When Carlyle complained, the neighbour pointed out that the cock crowed only two or at most three times a day. 'But,' said Carlyle, 'if you only knew what I suffer waiting for that cock to crow.' I am sure we all know people like that, harassed and anxious folk always waiting for something disastrous to happen.

In the Glasgow of my boyhood 'Wood and Selby' was a popular large city store. Many assumed it was owned by a Mr Wood and a Mr Selby, but in fact they were both the same person. Shortly after Mr Wood started in business, he found himself being pressurised into making quick decisions which he later found were sometimes unwise. So he invented a fictitious partner, named because he loved to holiday in Selby. Had he gone to Stirling on holiday, he might have called the shop Wood and Stirling. Thereafter whenever he had a difficult decision to make, he played for time by saying he would have to consult Mr Selby, his wiser self. I suppose when people say we should count up to ten when angry or hurt, they are in effect saying that we should stop and consult our wiser self.

The Chief Rabbi, Jonathan Sacks, tells how Sir Moses Montefiore, the distinguished 19th-century Jew, was once asked how much he was worth? The wealthy philanthropist thought for a little and then named a figure. The questioner replied, 'That cannot possibly be right. It is a large sum, but by my calculations you must be worth much more than that.' Sir Moses' reply was both wise and moving: 'You did not ask me how much I own. You asked me how much I am worth. So I calculated the amount

I have given to help others this year, and that is the figure I gave you. You see our real worth is what we are willing to share with others.'

Two bachelors were one day chatting before a football match. One complained that his elderly aunts would come up to him at weddings, poke him in the ribs and say, 'You'll be next.' His mate said, 'I used to have the same problem, but they stopped when I jokingly said the same thing to them one day at a funeral.'

A mother was waiting at the driving test centre while her son was sitting his test. From his glum expression she knew that he had failed. Inquiring of the examiner what had gone wrong, he said her son had failed to stop at a red light. Being particularly defensive of her son, she asked, 'But just how red was the light?'

Frank Szymanski was a famous American College footballer of bygone days. On one occasion he was called as a witness in a civil lawsuit. When, to Frank's surprise, the judge began by asking him how good a football player he actually was, he squirmed a little but finally said, 'Sir, I am the best centre Notre Dame College has ever had.' His coach, who happened to be present in the courtroom, was surprised to hear Frank say this, for he was normally a modest and unassuming person. When the proceedings ended, the coach asked Szymanski what had prompted him to make this claim. The player blushed and said, 'I hated doing it. But after all I was under oath to tell the truth.'

A Mr Cerf tells of a bus journey he once made. Near to him sat an old man holding a bunch of flowers. Across the aisle was a young woman gazing at the beautiful flowers he was carrying. As he was leaving the bus, the old man said to the woman, 'I can see you love flowers. I am sure my wife would like you to have them.' Before she could recover from the surprise, before she could say anything, the old man was gone. Tears came to her eyes when she saw him get off the bus and walk through the cemetery gates.